ORDNANCE SURVEY
LEISURE GUIDE

COTSWOLDS

**Produced jointly by the Publishing Division of the
Automobile Association and the Ordnance Survey**

Cover: Upper Slaughter Post Office

Title page: Houses at Upper Slaughter

Opposite: The house of Robert Raikes, the founder of the Sunday School movement, Gloucester

Introductory page: The cast-iron pump at Chipping Campden is dated 1832

Editor: Betty Sheldrick

Art Editor: M A Preedy MSIAD

Editorial contributors: Ruth Briggs (The Cotswold Countryside and Directory) Dr Philip Dixon MA, DPhil., FSA (The Ancient Cotswolds and Roman Roads, Towns and Villages) Ted Fryer (What are the Cotswolds? Managing the Landscape and The Cotswold Way), June Lewis (Cotswold Villages and A to Z Gazetteer), Mark Richards (Walks in the Cotswolds). Short features: Barbara Blatchley, Dr Philip Dixon MA, DPhil., FSA, Ted Fryer, June Lewis.

Picture researcher: Wyn Voysey

Original photography: S & O Mathews

Printed in Great Britain by Purnell Book Production Limited. Member of the BPCC Group.

Maps extracted from the Ordnance Survey's 1:63,360 Tourist Series, 1:25,000 Pathfinder Series and 1:250,000 Routemaster Series, with the permission of Her Majesty's Stationery Office. Crown Copyright reserved.

Additions to the maps by the Cartographic Dept of The Automobile Association and the Ordnance Survey.

Produced by the Publishing Division of The Automobile Association.

Distributed in the United Kingdom by the Ordnance Survey, Southampton, and the Publishing Division of The Automobile Association, Fanum House, Basingstoke, Hampshire RG21 2EA.

The contents of this publication are believed correct at the time of printing. Nevertheless, the Publishers cannot accept responsibility for errors or omissions, or for changes in details given.

Reprinted 1987, 1988
First Edition 1986

AA ISBN 0 86145 270 4 (softback)
AA ISBN 0 86145 349 2 (hardback)
OS ISBN 0 319 00048 6 (softback)
OS ISBN 0 319 00047 8 (hardback)

Published by The Automobile Association and the Ordnance Survey.

AA Reference: 58722 (softback)
AA Reference: 58748 (hardback)

COTSWOLDS

Contents

Using this Book

The entries in the Gazetteer have been carefully selected to reflect the interest and variety of the Cotswolds. For reasons of space, it has not been possible to include every community in the region. Certain towns, like Bath, for example, which are not strictly within the Cotswolds, have been included because of their outstanding importance to the cultural and social life of the area as a whole.

Each entry in the A to Z Gazetteer has the atlas page number on which the place can be found and/or its National Grid reference included under the heading. An explanation of how to use the National Grid is given on page 76.

Beneath many of the entries in the Gazetteer are listed AA-recommended hotels, guesthouses, garages and self-catering accommodation in the immediate vicinity of the place described. Hotels are also given an AA classification.

Please note: This guide lists only AA-appointed hotels selected for Special Merit Awards. For a full selection of AA-recommended hotels, please consult the AA guide, *Hotels and Restaurants in Britain*.

HOTELS

1-star	Good hotels and inns, generally of small scale and with good furnishings and facilities.
2-star	Hotels with a higher standard of accommodation. There should be 20% private bathrooms or showers.
3-star	Well-appointed hotels. Two-thirds of the bedrooms should have private bathrooms or showers.
4-star	Exceptionally well-appointed hotels offering high standards of comfort and service. All bedrooms should have private bathrooms or showers.
5-star	Luxury hotels offering the highest international standards.

Hotels often satisfy *some* of the requirements for higher classifications than that awarded.

Red-star	Red stars denote hotels which are considered to be of outstanding merit within their classification.
Country House Hotel	A hotel where a relaxed informal atmosphere prevails. Some of the facilities may differ from those at urban hotels of the same classification.

GUESTHOUSES

These are different from, but not necessarily inferior to, AA-appointed hotels, and they offer an alternative for those who prefer inexpensive and not too elaborate accommodation. They all provide clean, comfortable accommodation in homely surroundings. Each establishment must usually offer at least six bedrooms and there should be a general bathroom and a general toilet for every six bedrooms without private facilities.

Parking facilities should be reasonably close.

Other requirements include:
Well maintained exterior; clean and hygenic kitchens; good standard of furnishing; friendly and courteous service; access at reasonable times; the use of a telephone and full English breakfast.

A full selection of guesthouses in the area is provided in the AA's annual guide *Guesthouses, Farmhouses and Inns in Britain*.

SELF CATERING

These establishments, which are all inspected on a regular basis, have to meet minimum standards in accommodation, furniture, fixtures and fittings, services and linen.

Details are to be found in the AA annual guide *Holiday Homes, Cottages and Apartments in Britain*, which also contains a full selection of self-catering accommodation where indicated in the gazetteer section of this book.

TELEPHONE NUMBERS

Unless otherwise stated the telephone exchange is that of the town under which the establishment is listed. Where the exchange for a particular establishment is not that of the town under which it appears, the name of the exchange is given before the number. In some areas telephone numbers are likely to be changed by the telephone authorities during the currency of this publication. In case of difficulty check with the operator.

COTSWOLDS
Introduction

The Cotswolds, with their distinctive village architecture and enchanting landscape, are an enduring microcosm of Britain's past. Reaching back to Roman times and beyond, they have in more recent times become a popular tourist haunt. This book will help to enhance the pleasures of a visit, guiding the visitor through the history, traditions and wildlife of the Cotswolds. It lists and describes their towns and villages, marking out the routes of walks and motor tours which seek out the hidden corners and the finest scenery. Written entirely by people who live or work in the Cotswolds, and backed by the AA's research expertise and the Ordnance Survey's mapping, this guide is as useful to the faithful who return to the Cotswolds year after year as to the first-time visitor.

What are the Cotswolds?

From the Dorset coast to Yorkshire in the north lies a belt of oolitic limestone, laid down in ancient seas. At the widest part, where the land has been tilted up on its western side to form an escarpment with a gentle dip slope to the east, is the area known as the Cotswolds. It lies mainly in Gloucestershire and covers an area of 600-odd miles.

To today's visitors 'Cotswold' means warm-coloured stone, satisfying architecture, a feeling of peace, comfort and well-being, an upland landscape – but tamed. But former travellers from Shakespeare to William Cobbett and Sydney Smith found the hills wild, bleak and wearisome.

Country living may have been simple but not necessarily idyllic, if we are to believe the following catalogue of tasks from an 11th-century manuscript (mentioned in the Cotswold Countryside Collection at Northleach).

'In May, June and July men must harrow, spread manure, set up hurdles, shear the sheep, make good the fences and buildings, cut wood, clear the ground of weeds, make sheep pens, construct fish weirs and mills. During the next three months they reap, mow, set woad in the dibble, thatch and cover the crops, clean out the folds, prepare the sheep pens and pig sties and ploughs. During the winter they plough, in frosty weather split timber, prepare orchards, put the cattle in stalls and the pigs in sties, set up a drying oven on the threshing floor, and provide a hen roost. Finally in spring they graft, sow beans, set a vineyard, make ditches, hew wood to keep out the wild deer, set madder, sow flax and woad, and plant the vegetable garden.'

It was the Industrial Revolution which created such unpleasant urban conditions that places like the Cotswolds appeared to contain a sanity fast disappearing in the cities. As the 19th century turned into the 20th many people wanted to 'get

away from it all'. Community life held its attractions then as now – a mirage of simple country living.

In 1892 Ernest Gimson, who trained as an architect in Leicester and London, and his friends, the architects Sidney and Ernest Barnsley, moved to Sapperton, where they felt that building and the crafts, cabinet-making and blacksmithing for instance, could be combined in a way not possible in the usual urban architectural practice. They produced furniture of splendid design and craftsmanship and also built the village hall. This is an excellent example of keeping to the old style, making it blend with its neighbours almost to the point of being unnoticeable. Some of the original furnishings are inside.

C R Ashbee brought his Guild of Handicrafts– a previous generation of London's East-Enders – to Chipping Camden in 1902. It lasted a few years before it broke up but had a considerable influence. One workshop still survives today, run by a grandson of one of the founding members.

With the decline of the woollen industry in the first half of the 18th century and, later, the growing mechanisation of agriculture, people moved off the land into often more lucrative employment in the cities. Motor-cars have taken over from footpaths as the country dwellers' route to work or to their relatives in the next village. In searching for our rural roots, we can now experience the delights which our country forebears created but were not always able to enjoy. And what are those delights? Here are just a few.

High vistas and river valleys
Views across miles of rolling upland in all directions. Some high points advertise the distances you can see – on a clear day! From Broadway Tower it is said you can see 12 counties (13 before the local government reorganisation in 1974) – southwards across the Thames valley to the Wessex Downs; south-west to the Mendips; west to Wales; north-west to the Malverns and the Clee Hills in Shropshire. On a clear winter day with the sun low in the sky, the light reflects from blocks of flats on the southern edge of Birmingham. A pair of binoculars provides a view of these blocks looking like a futuristic army marching towards the Cotswolds.

Walkers take a break and enjoy the view towards Crickley Hill.

From wide vistas to the more intimate enclosed view. The Isbourne rises on the wilder slopes of Cleeve Common and winds its way northwards through Winchcombe to Shakespeare's Avon.

The Frome cuts its way from south of Witcombe Woods, through the remoter farms and woodlands around Miserden and westwards into the industrialised Golden Valley. On its way to Stroud it passes almost alpine settlements on the steep hillsides.

The watershed between the Thames and the Severn lies along the western scarp, so most rivers run eastwards to the Thames. The Bristol Avon rises, like its Thames-bound sisters, and flows eastwards through the Cotswold villages of Sherston and Easton Grey. It then leaves the hills to follow a clockwise turn through Malmesbury, Chippenham and Melksham before returning at Bradford-on-Avon and the Limpley Stoke valley near Bath.

The Thames tributaries of Evenlode, Windrush, Leach, Coln and Churn will reward the visitor with secluded villages and winding valleys with more open expanses on the plateaux above.

Seven Springs near Cheltenham is the source of the Churn and is, in fact, the remotest source of the Thames. However, the commemorative stone in a field to the north of Kemble and the Foss Way proclaims that spot as the official underground source. The statue, replaced by the stone, has now been removed to St John's Lock near Lechlade.

Tracks

The Cotswolds have a long history of settlement, and it is interesting to discover how our ancestors used to get from place to place.

Prehistoric routes can be traced, such as the one we now call the Jurassic Way from the south-west to the north-east. It links many important places of the day such as the Rollright Stones near Long Compton and the Stone and Iron Age hill-forts of Crickley Hill. Later the Romans imposed their road system, which was so good that much of it lies under our present-day tarmac roads. However, to the east of Tetbury there are parts of the Foss Way which did not comply with the requirements of later times and so reverted to tracks, which make good footpaths for us now.

There are tracks for special uses, such as saltways. Look on the map for Salter's Hill, Saltway Farm, Saltridge. A major route (from which others diverged) from Droitwich to the Thames valley crosses the Cotswolds between Hailes and Lechlade. It is mostly tarmacked and can be travelled by car. Other tracks were used as drove roads for animals, or for medieval 'wool trains' of packhorses carrying wool from the Cotswolds to the Continent.

With the big thrust to improve the roads in the 18th century came the turnpikes. Toll-houses are still a familiar sight with their windows which allow the turnpike keeper to look along the road in each direction. One such house to the north of Bishop's Cleeve still displays the charges. Like motorway developments today, turnpikes were not always appreciated at first. Nash in his account of Worcestershire (1799) relates:

'It is not surprising that when turnpikes were first erected, and tolls taken, that the common people should be disgusted and riotous, but after some few persons had been executed for cutting down turnpikes at Ledbury and Tewkesbury, the farmers and gentry finding the roads gradually mended, the aversion subsided, and all were contented.'

Architecture

The Cotswold vernacular is a type of architecture that has evolved within the Cotswold region over the centuries rather than sprung up in response to fashion. It is difficult to define precisely, but if you think of an accent or a dialect as the speech peculiar to a district, then the vernacular style is the architectural equivalent. It is the architecture of the indigenous craftsman, based on local tradition, suited to the needs and character of the inhabitants, taking into account the climate and social conditions, and using the building materials of the region.

Of the grander buildings that reflect the vernacular, Owlpen, south of Stroud, is a beautiful example of a Cotswold Elizabethan manor-house. Late 17th-century style is evident at Dyrham Park, a National Trust property, and 18th-century classical at Dodington Park.

Owlpen Manor and its church nestle into a hollow of the wooded hillside.

Batsford Park, just north-west of Moreton-in-Marsh, is a good example of a 19th-century Cotswold Tudor mansion, and Rodmarton, built by Ernest Barnsley, is representative of the 20th century. By contrast, Sezincote has an exotic flavour, with its onion dome said to be the inspiration for the Brighton Pavilion.

If simpler buildings take your fancy, Chipping Campden, Marshfield, Northleach and Wotton-under-Edge have outstanding almshouses, which proliferated in the 17th century. The bus shelters at Farmington and Nympsfield are also worth a visit.

The latest buildings are often of artificial stone as the villages expand to become, to some extent, outlying commuter suburbs of many cities.

Churches

There is endless enjoyment in these monuments to social change, let alone religious significance. Walk down the naves of St James at Chipping Campden and St Peter and St Paul at Northleach and you may well conclude that they were designed by the same person. The stained glass at Fairford is a marvel. Gargoyles in wood and stone, such as the imp on the choir screen at Winchcombe, illustrates the humour of the sculptors as well as their skill. Misericords under choir seats in some churches show scenes of medieval life.

The brasses at Fairford, Northleach and Campden tell stories about the notable locals, such as wool merchants. Brass-rubbing is an enjoyable pastime, but always ask permission first. Some churches augment their income by charging a fee, while others prohibit rubbing because of wear and tear. Substitute copies at brass-rubbing centres still produce excellent examples to remind you of your visit.

Festivals and customs

Cotswold towns and villages have many celebrations, fetes, flower festivals and open days during the year. Here are some with more ancient backgrounds.

Dover's Hill, above Chipping Campden, is the scene for Dover's Games, a modern-day revival of Robert Dover's Cotswold Olympicks dating from James I's time. Apart from the fun of the event, including shin-kicking, the torchlight procession is unforgettable.
Cooper's Hill, near Brockworth, has a slope of

Cheese-rolling contest at Cooper's Hill.

one-in-one. What better place to chase Double Gloucester cheeses from the maypole at the top to the St John Ambulance waiting at the bottom! This is a hair-raising entertainment for Spring Bank Holiday Monday.
Cranham has a feast and a deer roast in August.

At Bisley on Ascension Day the wells are dressed with garlands of flowers.

Bisley has seven wells issuing from a decorative stone well-head set in a bank. On Ascension Day the wells are dressed. Although this was inspired by the Derbyshire custom 100 years ago, do not expect to see pictures made of flower petals pressed into wet clay. This is more a garlanding of the well-heads but delightful all the same.
Painswick church is encircled by children clasping hands in the old Clipping Ceremony in September. This clipping has nothing to do with the yew trees in the churchyard, but comes from the Old English word meaning 'clasping'.
Marshfield's group of Mummers perform their age-old play on Boxing Day each year – in the snow if necessary.

Visitors to the Cotswolds

The Cotswolds as yet do not suffer in general from the tourist pressures experienced in places like the Lake District, Snowdonia and the West Country. In the West Country, tourists are sometimes known as 'grockles' – a term which implies that they, the visitors, are coming to make life worse for us, the locals. It is a pity that the scenic and commercial attractions of parts of our country can create pressures which provoke an adverse reaction. Ideally then, visitors should treat the places they visit thoughtfully and leave them unmarked, as though they had never been there.

Most people do. They do it by making an effort to understand the life of the place. They avoid walking through a field of corn or mowing-grass four abreast because it reduces the crop and the farmer's income. They remove all traces of their picnics. They admire drystone walls and think of the sweat, toil and skill which erected such cattle- and sheep-proof barriers. They do not climb over them nor take chunks for souvenirs or rockeries, even if the walls are decaying.

Occasionally, they whisper a momentary thank-you to the unknown people who put a footbridge in, built a stile, opened a pub, filled a pothole, trimmed a hedge, made a lay-by, put up the signposts – and are patient when they have to drive slowly for a mile behind a muck-spreader! In other words they follow the short country code:

Take nothing but photographs
Leave nothing but footprints
Kill nothing but time.

To those with such an awareness and the capacity to slow down will come the reward of welcome and the parting farewell of 'Do come back' – over and over again.

The Ancient Cotswolds

The orchis, trefoil, harebells nod all day,
High above Gloucester and the Severn Plain.
Few come there, where the curlew ever and again
Cries faintly, and no traveller makes stay,
Since steep the road is,
And the villages
Hidden by hedges wonderful in May.

The interior of Hetty Pegler's Tump, named after the wife of a 17th-century landowner.

To the Gloucester poet, Ivor Gurney, the Cotswold landscape was a high edge, dotted with windswept copses, and threaded by remote valleys in which hamlets sheltered. Today we can look down from this edge on the towns and fields of the fertile Severn Valley.

The ancient view was very different. Pollen from the peat near the Severn suggests that the valley was heavily wooded between the Ice Ages until widespread clearances began about 2,000 BC. Among the trees there were clearings, confined perhaps to the banks of alluvial gravel, from which Old Stone Age flint tools have been recovered. After the last Ice Age, about 10,000 BC, the Cotswold uplands were more lightly wooded. Trees grew steadily thicker on the hills until forest clearance marked the beginning of farming and settlement a little before 3,000 BC.

Cairns and mounds

The most obvious relics left behind by these New Stone Age people are the long barrows, 70 of which lie in the central Cotswolds. These are huge cairns of stones, carefully built with internal passages, roofed chambers, and drystone-faced walls. Their construction is estimated to have taken as much as 15,000 man-hours each – a huge amount of labour in a society of subsistence farmers. Though bodies are found within them, they were not cemeteries as we would understand them, for the number of dead in each is normally small; nor are they, like the Egyptian pyramids, the revered tombs of kings, for the broken-up skeletons within them were piled together, to our eyes with small respect. They were perhaps places of ritual, designed to preserve and control the powers of the mighty dead. Two are particularly worth visiting in this area: Belas Knap, a little to the south of Winchcombe, and Hetty Pegler's Tump, near Stroud; both are now low, grass-covered stone mounds, with narrow stone-roofed chambers entered by low passages. When newly built, they must have caught the eye of the traveller on the skyline, great gashes of white limestone as obtrusive as a motorway viaduct.

The people who built them had recently taken to farming. They were now settling down on the land and not just living off it by hunting and fruit- and berry-gathering. Once it was thought that they formed small communes, having only peaceful contacts with each other – the exchange of flint or hard stone for tools. Discoveries in southern England over the past few years have told a different story, for New Stone Age villages, long looked for, are now being excavated and are proving to be strongly defended. Near Birdlip on the Cotswold edge, in the Country Park at Crickley Hill, the final Stone Age settlement was fiercely attacked by men using flint-tipped arrows, and then burnt – houses, shrine,

The Cotswolds are dotted with Stone Age long barrows. Trees delineate this one at Coberley.

defences and all. Some of the five earlier villages on this site, too, may have suffered a similar fate, for each showed clear signs of burning.

Though their lives were beset by superstitions, our Stone Age ancestors were people who are recognisably modern – gathered into groups under leaders capable of commanding major building programmes, jealous of their rights, and envious of the possessions of others. It is striking that estimates of the dead buried in long barrows would allow no more than some 200 per generation for the whole country. Whoever these dead were – chieftains, priests perhaps most likely – they were a highly select group of individuals.

The Bronze Age and its barrows

Among the obscure terms which travellers will find on their maps is the word 'tumulus'. In most cases the visitor will find a low circular burial mound, a round barrow, often now capped by a small coppice of trees. Over 350 of these are known in the Gloucestershire Cotswolds. Some can be seen only from the air. Others, like those at Wyck Rissington near Bourton-on-the-Water or North Cerney barrow near Cirencester, remain obvious landmarks.

To a much greater extent than the Stone Age long barrows they lie in clusters. This is particularly clear in the groups near Lechlade and near Upper Swell, to the north-west of Stow-in-the-Wold. At Condicote, are the remains of a *henge*, a huge circular earthwork, which was used for rituals early in the Bronze Age (at about the time of Abraham), ar.d both long barrows and round burial mounds appear to be concentrated around it.

Where they have been excavated these round barrows normally cover a cremation burial in a pit, with occasional subsidiary cremations dug into the mound. It is likely that they were the burials of prominent individuals, and the clusters may be the cemeteries of such people over several generations, but where they lived is one of the great mysteries of this period. Elsewhere in England a few small villages of circular wooden buildings belong to this age of round barrows. Nothing of the kind is yet known from the Cotswolds, and the old joke, that the Bronze Age never lived, still holds true in this area. But the profusion of barrows in the hills, and the scatter of Bronze Age axes, daggers and spearheads, turned up by chance by the plough, show that it can be only a matter of time before their villages are identified.

The age of hill-forts

The Cotswold edge bristles with the remains of fortresses, the majority of which belong to the Iron Age, from about 600 BC. Even in ruins they are impressive, enclosing areas up to 100 acres in extent. Their banks are now gently sloping, grass-covered mounds, but, below the turf, excavations reveal tall, vertical drystone walls, whose effect was accentuated by rock-cut ditches. Their interiors today are featureless, to the extent that some have thought of them as cattle enclosures. Those that have been dug, however, have produced the remains of round and rectangular timber buildings and of burning and destruction, which hints at the motives which led Iron Age

Ritual stone circle and sacrificial slab excavated by volunteers at Crickley Hill.

rulers to protect their settlements with massive defences.

Some hill-forts are very large. That on Nottingham Hill, north-east of Cheltenham, at over 100 acres is one of the biggest in the country. Nearby at Conderton near Bredon is a tiny affair of only three acres. It seems certain that they must have had different functions. The large enclosures were perhaps tribal and marketing centres, and corrals for cattle; the smaller ones were probably the fortified residences of petty chieftains. In some cases we can see that different shapes are due to differences in date. The single-banked forts at Leckhampton and Crickley are of the 5th century BC. The magnificent tiers of ramparts which surround the hill at Painswick Beacon are probably four centuries later, belonging to a time of increasing tension between tribes, as smaller groups were being swallowed up to form major tribes in the last few generations of independence before the Roman Conquest.

The hill-forts tell only part of the story. Many, perhaps most, of the inhabitants of Iron Age Britain lived in the unfortified villages and farmsteads whose circular houses and fenced enclosures are a regular feature on aerial photographs. On the ground they are almost invisible and rarely worth a visit, but when excavated they provide a fascinating picture of life during the last few centuries BC. One such settlement, in the gravel pits at Beckford near Tewkesbury, revealed a regular pattern of rectangular, fenced yards, which were arranged beside a street and contained the remains of houses, and of rubbish- and storage-pits. A few of these settlements owed their origin to some natural resource – iron ore or salt – but most were agricultural communities of a dozen or so families.

From these small beginnings tribal centres were developing into towns in the last few years BC and the first years of our era, and relics of the growth are preserved in the Cotswolds. At Salmonsbury beside Bourton-on-the-Water a large 56-acre enclosure was found to be densely occupied from the numbers of round houses discovered there. Sitting as it does on a low-lying gravel bank and not high on a hill, Salmonsbury gives the impression of an early town rather than a hill-fort. A little to the north of Cirencester, near the village of Bagendon, is a perplexing series of banks and ditches which cut off an area of huge size – about 500 acres. Digging here has revealed some scattered occupation and has shown that in one part of the site lay a mint, producing that novelty from the Continent – coinage. This suggests that the area was politically important, a tribal capital, and gives us our first evidence for the name of the tribe who dominated the Cotswolds – the *Dobunni*.

A glimpse of the wealth of the chiefs of this age was revealed by accident over 100 years ago, when quarrymen came across a richly-adorned female burial on Barrow Wake near Birdlip. The objects, now to be seen in Gloucester City Museum, included bronze bowls, a silver gilt brooch, a decorated bucket, and one of that splendid series of highly-ornamented bronze mirrors which have been found scattered across southern Britain and which belong to the last years BC or the first few years AD. The Birdlip lady must have been one of the highest rank in her society. Who she actually was and where she lived are both quite unknown, but she is among the first of the prehistoric peoples of the Cotswolds who have a shadowy sort of identity.

Epilogue

Almost the whole of mankind's past is prehistoric, and little is known from written sources about Britain until the Roman period, a mere 2,000 years ago. Our knowledge about the previous hundreds of thousands of years of development and change has increased to an astonishing degree thanks to the careful investigations of the last two or three generations. We can now hold an axe made 50,000 years ago, or stand in the roadways of a defended village of the New Stone Age 5,000 years old, or touch the charred grains of barley last seen by an Iron Age farmer when he put them into his granary in 500 BC. Trade, warfare, and social relations may be guessed at by looking at the debris of the past, but, to an extent that historians and others accustomed to the written word find hard to imagine, the people themselves elude us.

Much of mankind's life is built on hope and its richest experience enhanced by story and song, but as far as prehistoric peoples are concerned their motives and hopes are lost, and we can hardly even imagine what they really felt when, like us, they stood in their then newly-built settlements on the Cotswold edge and gazed across the broad vale of the Severn.

The delicately-engraved bronze Birdlip Mirror, crafted during the Iron Age and now in Gloucester City Museum.

The Cotswold Countryside

A stonechat pauses with a beakful of food. These handsome birds prefer uncultivated land.

Origins

While the wide range of wildlife and scenery in the hills is the result of a variety of influences, the most fundamental of these is that of their geological structure. Some 180 million years ago the area we now know as the Cotswolds was under a shallow sea. For several millennia sediments composed of clay, sand and shell fragments were deposited on the sea floor and these accumulated to form the limestones that give us the hills of today. The famous oolitic limestones (so called after the spherical grains, or oolites, of which they are composed) form some of the finest building stone in the country and contribute to the special character of the Cotswold villages, farms and drystone walls. Some of the rock layers are highly fossiliferous and provide a clear indication of the prehistoric fauna and flora of the Cotswolds.

The relief of the Cotswolds is dominated by its steep scarp slope in the west. The highest point is at Cleeve Hill, north of Cheltenham, where 330 metres is reached. The gentle dip slope drops away to the south-east and it is here that many of the rivers rise and begin their course to link ultimately with the Thames.

Once the last ice sheets retreated some 10,000 years ago, plant and animal life began to colonise the hills. The natural vegetation of the Cotswolds would undoubtedly have been deciduous woodland, a very different landscape from that of today. As soon as human beings arrived, in Neolithic times, clearings were made in the forest. With the ensuing evolution of agriculture and growth of the population more and more of the woodland disappeared, giving way eventually to extensive tracts of rough grazing land. Changes continue to the present day and over recent decades the sheepwalks have given way to a landscape of more intensive agriculture.

Habitats

The combined effects of geology, climate, topography, soils, land-use history and present-day management give rise to the variety of habitats and wildlife that epitomise the Cotswold countryside. Farmland predominates with its acres of wheat, barley, oats, oil-seed rape, vegetables and grass leys (seeded pastures). Interspersed between the fields are tracks, hedges, walls and verges, all providing cover and food for their own range of wildlife.

Most woodland is concentrated on the steep slopes of the scarp. Elsewhere, on the dip slope the woods are smaller, though with some notably large exceptions, such as the forests of Chedworth and Withington, and Cirencester Park. Individual trees too are important in the landscape – they are the home of small wild animals, act as shelter for livestock and also have value as timber. Thickets of thorn, rose and elderberry grow on some of the steeper pastures and provide feeding, roosting and nesting sites for birds such as yellowhammer and stonechat.

Here and there, remnants of the once widespread sheep pastures remain, unaffected by plough, herbicide or artificial fertiliser. These famous Cotswold grasslands support a wealth of wildlife.

The young of the yellowhammer demanding food. The female builds the nest of dried grass and lines it with finer grass and hair.

Some of the Cotswold valleys are dry, indicative of an earlier, wetter climate, while others have small clear streams flowing through them. In some places, for example near the village of Barnsley, the stream is a winterbourne, flowing only in the winter when the water-table is high. Associated with the streams and springs may be small patches of marshy ground; where left undrained these support a variety of sedges and rushes, attractive flowers like marsh orchids and the amphibious frogs and toads.

Cotswold woodlands

Several different types of woodland habitat are to be found on the Cotswolds – old and new, broadleaved and evergreen. Surviving stretches of the ancient forest are found most frequently on the steepest hillsides. Although managed for timber they retain a truly native woodland vegetation and are the richest woods for wildlife. Beech, ash and oak are the commonest trees, complemented by yew, cherry, whitebeam, sycamore, holly and hazel, to name just a few. The forest floor is a patchwork of plants, sometimes carpets of bluebells, elsewhere extensive sheets of dog's mercury with its tiny green February flowers, or drifts of white ramsons scenting the air with garlic. Primroses are found along the tracks and are accompanied in spring by the delicate flowers of the wood anemone and wood sorrel.

Badgers are still common in the woods, although with their shy nocturnal habits are rarely seen. Fallow deer inhabit some of the larger woods, while the grey squirrel is ubiquitous. Foxes, small mice and voles add to the mammalian fauna of the woods.

Bird life can also be rich and varied, particularly where there is a good mixture of tree and shrub species and different ages of vegetation. Woodpeckers, titmice and finches

A tawny owl carries its prey back to its nest in the hole of a tree. It feeds on small mammals – mice, voles, young rats and shrews.

may be abundant and in springtime the air is filled with the songs of warblers such as chiff-chaffs, blackcaps, garden and wood warblers. There are winter visitors to the woods too, notably the large flocks of brambling from Scandinavia, which come to feast on the fallen beech mast (seeds). Tawny owls, sparrowhawks and buzzards may all be seen from time to time in the larger woods.

Cotswold grasslands

Once, the Cotswolds were dominated by rough grazing land, and even as recently as 50 years ago about half the area was under permanent pasture. Since the last War, however, there has been a dramatic reduction in the acreage of such land, so that today the ancient grasslands occupy but a tiny fraction of the overall area of the Cotswolds. These are either the steepest slopes of the valleys, impractical to plough, or the common lands, which, with their traditional rights of grazing held by local residents, have survived the agricultural changes taking place around them. Places such as Cleeve Common near Cheltenham or Minchinhampton and Rodborough Commons near Stroud include examples of this ancient, unimproved, calcareous grassland habitat.

Upwards of some 150 different species of grasses and flowering herbs may be found on a

Early purple orchids have long been associated with love and reproduction. They were used as a love potion and also for determining the sex of children.

Bird's-foot-trefoil is found in bright abundance on roadsides, pastures and grasslands.

single ancient common – the attractive quaking grass, purple thyme and knapweeds, yellow cowslips, rockrose, bird's-foot-trefoil and kidney vetch, white ox-eye daisies, blue harebells and scabious all combine to give a spangled beauty throughout the summer and autumn. The commons are famous too for their orchids – early purple and green-winged orchids in May, then bee, frog, fragrant, common spotted and pyramidal orchids in high summer.

Butterflies and other insects thrive on the diverse mixture of plant species and feed on the flowers. Specialities are the chalkhill and small blue butterflies, the marbled white and grayling. Common blue, green hairstreak, meadow brown and skippers are also resident, while visitors may

The peacock butterfly bluffs predatory birds by displaying its wings with their eye-like markings.

include the colourful peacock, painted lady and clouded yellow.

The key to the protection of these valuable grassland areas is their continued grazing by sheep or cattle to maintain their open character. Where there is insufficient grazing, shrubs like hawthorn, rose and dogwood encroach and could ultimately shade out the grassland flowers altogether. Thus in some areas scrub is cut back to ensure that a range of habitats is maintained and the maximum diversity of wildlife encouraged. At Painswick Beacon, for example, an unusual feature is the spread of Scots Pine across the once open hillside, and careful management is necessary to maintain the best areas of grassland while preserving some of the trees.

Rivers and streams

The main rivers of the Cotswolds – the Evenlode, Dikler, Windrush, Coln and Churn – rise from springs near the scarp and flow south-eastwards across the inclined plateau towards the valley of the Thames. The Thames itself rises in the Cotswolds, its source marked on the map at Thames Head not far from Cirencester.

The character of the streams owes much to the calcareous limestone over which they flow. Clear, sparkling water rippling over a stony bed is typical even in villages such as the Slaughters and Bourton-on-the-Water where the streams are an intrinsic part of the village scene.

Dragonflies and dainty blue damselflies are plentiful along the streams and alight on marginal reed grass and yellow flags. Long stretches of river are covered in summer with the attractive white flowers of the water crowfoot, a member of the buttercup family, while the banks may be overhung with alder and sallow. Otters once frequented the streams but have now sadly died out. Just occasionally one may be sighted journeying through the area, but more commonly nowadays it is mink which are spotted along the rivers.

Cotswold Water Park

By far the most extensive wetland area in the Cotswolds is the series of 100 lakes lying in two distinct areas south and east of Cirencester at the foot of the hills. The Cotswold Water Park is an entirely man-made habitat, the lakes having been formed as a result of some 60 years of gravel extraction in this uppermost part of the Thames Valley. Digging still continues, so more lakes are being created all the time. The area has become a major tourist attraction, and its wildlife coexists with those using the lakes for recreational purposes.

The alkaline nature of the water in the disused gravel pits is derived from the underlying calcareous limestone and gravel and gives rise to the characteristic features of such marl lakes – exceptionally clear blue waters, little algal growth and a diverse range of aquatic wildlife. The older lakes have become well colonised with marginal reeds and shrubs. Their wildlife interest is greatest where there are islands, inlets and shallow, shelving banks. Here may be seen nesting kingfisher, sedge warbler, mute swan and great crested grebes with their incredible spring courtship display. The willow beds of the Water Park remain a stronghold for nightingales, whose melodious song can be heard during the spring and summer.

In the winter the Water Park becomes a mecca for birdwatchers, who flock to watch the thousands of wildfowl which migrate here from the far north. Tufted duck, pochard, teal and wigeon are plentiful while smaller numbers of shoveler, gadwall, goldeneye and goosander may be spotted.

Other habitats

Away from the woods, pastures and streams, the farmland of the Cotswolds supports a wide range of wildlife. Birds such as corn bunting, partridge and pheasant have long been associated with the fields. Poppies still occur from time to time in the cereal crops, and kestrels hover overhead in

search of harvest mice in the wheatfields.

The drystone walls, so typical of the Cotswolds, themselves provide nooks and crannies for nesting wrens and robins. Ivy-leaved toadflax and English stonecrop root in the crevices, and lizards bask in the sun. Hedges too, with their scattered trees, give cover for nesting birds and food for the huge winter flocks of fieldfare and redwing.

Disused railway cuttings run through parts of the Cotswolds and present another habitat for fauna and flora. Old quarries too may be of interest not only to the geologist but also to the botanist – rare plants such as the limestone fern and Cotswold pennycress may be found on scree slopes. Even the old stone mines, with their horizontal shafts running underground, harbour wildlife. With their even temperature and humidity they are ideal sites for hibernating bats in winter, and some contain the very rare greater horseshoe bat.

Nature reserves

The Cotswold Commons and Beechwoods National Nature Reserve near Painswick includes some of the finest beechwoods of the Cotswolds and is easily accessible along marked public paths. The National Trust administers Minchinhampton Common and Rodborough Common, both near Stroud, and a number of other nature reserves are protected by the County Trusts for Nature Conservation and again cover a wide range of habitats. Woodland at The Frith (SO 875085), grassland at Swift's Hill (SO 877067), lakes at Whelford Pools in the Cotswold Water Park (SU 174995) and a stretch of disused railway track near Chedworth Roman Villa (SP 051138) are among the variety of attractive sites which serve to show the visitor the full beauty of the Cotswold countryside and its wildlife.

A kingfisher on its fishing perch.

Managing the Landscape

Shaped by history

The landscape which attracts us today is only about 150 years old. This is a very short period compared with the 6,000 years since human beings first started making an impact on the Cotswolds.

The first settlers were hunter-gatherers who moved into the area about 5,000–6,000 BC, but it was the Neolithic peoples who made the first impression on the landscape some 2,000 years later. They were the first farmers and carried out systematic clearance of the light, easily-cultivated soils of the hills to plant their crops. They left some 85 tombs to bury their dead.

During the Bronze Age the population increased and by the Iron Age, around 500 BC, there were many signs of occupation of the Cotswolds including some 35 known defensive sites.

The Romans left their permanent stamp on the landscape with their legacy of roads, two of which (Foss Way and Ermin Way) are still important through routes today.

When the Saxons moved into the area around the 7th century, they probably took over existing settlements on the Cotswold plateau and established new ones on spring lines with a ready supply of water. The majority of Cotswold place names have Anglo-Saxon origins, and, by the end of the Saxon era, much of the land was in the ownership of the Church.

By the time of the Domesday Survey of 1086, a large area of the Cotswolds was already under cultivation, with woodland along the western escarpment. In the following centuries more woodland was cleared, and the open field system of arable farming was increased until a maximum was reached in the 14th century. This period saw the real beginnings of the Cotswold wool trade and the area of sheep pastures was greatly

Farmland near Dowdeswell. Before the 18th- and 19th-century Enclosure Acts this wold landscape would have been open sheep pasture.

increased, especially on ecclesiastical holdings.

After the Dissolution of the Monasteries in the 16th century, estates tended to be smaller. There was an upsurge in the building of Cotswold stone dwellings by country gentry and yeoman alike. The greatest landscape change occurred between 1700 and 1840 when at least 120,000 acres of open land were enclosed by Acts of Parliament. This gave rise to the familiar drystone walls and hedges dividing off the newly enclosed areas. Hunting and shooting became popular with the 'squirearchy' and many land-owners planted coverts and shelter belts for foxes and game birds.

Since the middle of the last century, the landscape has remained basically the same – predominantly agricultural, sprinkled with naturally integrated villages and farmsteads. In the last 40 years fundamental change has started again.

All these changes were made in response to needs felt by individuals, small groups, such as medieval merchants or a parish as a whole, big estates, municipalities or the whole nation. Food, shelter and warmth are vital needs. So fields were planted or grazed for food, trees felled and stone quarried for shelter, and more trees felled for warmth.

The methods appropriate to the time dictated how the land was used. Great sheep walks of scrub and grassland were managed by shepherds and their flocks. Woodlands were coppiced to ensure continuity of timber. Old field patterns with undulating ridge and furrow can be seen crossing the modern field boundaries. An ancient track can be detected by the way today's cornfield ripens earlier along its line.

Conservation and development

As the land was enclosed and formed into more efficient farming units to produce food more economically for an exploding population, so reaction set in on a national scale. There are now many organisations whose objectives are to retain the traditional landscape. The following are a few examples.

The Open Spaces Society was founded in 1865 to retain as much as possible of the country's open space, such as commons, and make them available for public use. Thirty years later three far-sighted people formed a National Trust to acquire land as the only reasonably sure way of protecting it. Now, after 90 years, it has vast property holdings and is the largest private landowner in the country. It is 'private' because it is not a government department. 'National' refers to its operation nationwide. It has many 'open space' properties in the Cotswolds open to the public at large without payment.

The Council for the Protection of Rural England was founded in 1926. It has fought on the political front on many occasions to ensure that major developments are carefully designed to blend into the countryside, or are even stopped if the apparent need can be proved to be false. Such developments are motorways, bypasses, airports, reservoirs, power stations, quarries and mines, as well as housing and industrial development in, for example, green belts.

The Ramblers' Association started in 1935 to preserve and enhance rights of way for the landless public. County naturalists' trusts were formed to acquire land for creating nature reserves. Of more recent foundation the Woodland Trust acquires woodlands in order to preserve their existence and manages them to maintain a continuity of tree cover.

Landowning and farming interests have also come to be represented nationally by the National Farmers' Union and the Country Landowners' Association.

Governments altered the face of the land by creating the Forestry Commission after the First World War and charged it with producing timber to reduce our national reliance on imports. This was inevitably a long-term project and, equally inevitably, early decisions taken, such as planting quick-growing conifers, were criticised later when thinking and opinions changed. There are a number of Commission woods in the Cotswolds, but in a wider context it has a great influence on private landholdings by offering grants for suitable schemes.

The need in time of war for home-produced food moved governments into subsidising farmers, and this has gone further with the control of agricultural policy being determined on a European, rather than a national basis. Introduce bigger and more efficient machinery and the farmer refashions the landscape by taking out hedgerows and drystone walls. Reduce farmers' milk production quotas and the landscape changes again to more corn, vegetables, sheep or oil-seed rape. The profit motive drives farmers just as much as it does production and sales managers in factories. The landscape is a workshop – but what a nice one!

The pressures on the countryside over the last 90 years prompted a number of measures, for example the curbing of ribbon development of houses and industries along main roads between

towns. Eventually a more comprehensive approach was adopted in the Town and Country Planning Acts, and particularly in the National Parks and Access to the Countryside Act, 1949. This was later followed by the Countryside Act, 1968 and the Wildlife and Countryside Act, 1981. Apart from the creation of the Nature Conservancy Council and the registration of rights of way, 10 National Parks were set up, and other, less wild, places were designated as 'areas of outstanding natural beauty'.

The Cotswolds were so designated in 1966. It is a compliment to the better side of human nature because most of the beauty is the result of our fashioning of these 600 square miles over the centuries. Designation of an 'area of outstanding natural beauty' gives strength to local authorities to adopt policies intended to encourage sympathetic development.

Planning ahead

The task of planners is to reconcile many competing interests for the use of land. Builders would jump at the chance of erecting large numbers of houses in this very 'desirable area'; accessible to London and the south-east, the Cotswolds would also be attractive to industrialists wishing to open new factories. Motorways, reservoirs, quarries, oil exploration – cases can be made for all these in the interest of improving facilities and providing employment.

Main picture: Sheep grazing near Bisley. Inset: Old farm buildings are put to good use to house small industries, like this ceramics workshop at Northleach.

Tourism could be further developed with the provision of more hotels, caravan sites, zoos, funfairs and widened roads. On the other hand, farmers and naturalists alike may object to the restoring of a footpath because of possible vandalism – either to crops or to rare plants – by the newcomers it would attract.

Reconciling interests is made more difficult by the fact that there are 14 local authorities with territory in the Cotswolds – five county councils and nine district councils. With so many people involved their views could well diverge and inconsistency result from different ways of treating development. To meet this a Joint Advisory Committee brings together local authorities and other interested bodies covering agriculture, tourism and conservation. This committee advises its constituent authorities on a common approach to problems and gives advice to developers, so that we do not destroy the very thing we wish to keep. From what may seem a boring 'dry-as-dust' committee atmosphere comes some protection of the view extending before you.

Major caravan developments have been refused. Rejection of an application for a zoo/funfair resulted in a stately home being sold after being 200 years in the same family. Redundant barns house small industries as at Northleach, or convert to dwellings. Standards of house designs are improved to blend with the old, even if modern materials are used. Farming can be shown to be compatible with conserving wildlife and yet continue to be profitable. Farmers are encouraged to offer bed and breakfast accommodation and so use existing capacity to house tourists. New roads are 'landscaped' and verges are planted with trees appropriate to the Cotswolds.

In several ways the authorities are trying to cope with the pressures imposed by economics and by a more leisured and travel-conscious society. Some parts of the country suffer far more than the Cotswolds from the influx of visitors. Let us hope that this region will be able to absorb the pressures so that the delights illustrated in this book will be available for a long time.

Roman Roads, Towns and Villas

To the motorist travelling between the East Midlands and the Cotswolds, the Foss Way may be no more than a straight and convenient bypass to the main roads which pass through Coventry, Stratford or Cheltenham. The road is mostly narrow, often hilly, and quiet by comparison with its broad neighbours. Few may know that it was once the principal highway across the newly-conquered province of Britain.

Above: The Foss Way near Castle Combe. Opposite: Chedworth Roman Villa is a well-preserved example of Roman country life.

The Cotswold roads

Roman armies landed late in the summer of AD 43, probably at Richborough in Kent and near Chichester in Sussex. After fighting their way across the Medway and the Thames and subduing the tribal centre at Colchester and the great hill-forts of Dorset, they incorporated the south and south-west of England into a new Roman province. Some areas remained native princedoms, notably Hampshire under the 'king and ally' Cogidumnus. Part at least of the Cotswold Dobunni had, it seems, surrendered to Rome before the final overthrow of their allies, and a series of military works was soon built across their territory. Among the earliest were fortresses at Cirencester (soon to become a major city some two miles south of the Dobunnic tribal centre of Bagendon) and at Kingsholm near Gloucester.

The road through Cirencester to Gloucester is perhaps the earliest in the region and provided a rapid route from the southern ports, via the new town at Silchester south of Reading, onwards to Usk in Gwent, where an outpost fortress was built during these opening stages of the invasion. In its southern section, from Silchester to Newbury, this roadline has been mostly abandoned. Minor roads beside the M4 on the Marlborough Downs now continue its course to Swindon, where the A419, today on top of the Roman road, runs north-westwards to pass to the east of Cricklade and arrive at Cirencester. Now called the Ermin Way, the Roman road continues as the A417 across the Cotswolds to Gloucester. From Swindon onwards this is a fascinating stretch to drive along, for one can see the way in which the surveyors laid a straight course from crest to crest, sometimes continuing directly across to the next rise and sometimes altering the line a few degrees to bring the road nearer to its destination.

From the south-west the Foss Way (now the A433 and the A429) is aligned straight towards Cirencester, and then bypasses the town on what is now a tree-fringed lane, to meet Ermin Way between Preston and Siddington, originally the southernmost point of the Foss Way. The military road-builders obviously expected heavy traffic up from the south on Ermin Way, around Cirencester and then north-eastwards along the Foss across the rising hills of the Cotswolds towards the large native settlement of Salmonsbury at Bourton-on-the-Water. From there the road runs almost completely straight, over a distance of some 60 miles to the tribal centre that preceded the Roman city of Leicester. The end of its course, after a further 50 miles, was the legionary fortress of Lincoln.

Over recent years aerial photographs and excavations have revealed a series of small forts in the Midlands along the line of the Foss. In our region a possible candidate is the fort at Dorn, to the north of Bourton-on-the-Water. These forts date from early in the invasion period, and it is now clear that the Foss Way was intended to be the spine of a defence system between Lincoln and Cirencester, a spine which connected military bases and outposts both to the north and to the south. The scheme was not to build a fixed frontier, like that later constructed as Hadrian's Wall between the Tyne and Solway, but to create a broad military zone serviced by a fast road, the Foss Way, and cut by north–south roads radiating from the south-east. Behind the protected area, the pacification and Romanisation of the new province could proceed in safety.

Some of these other roads can be followed most easily on foot, or by the motorist content to tolerate detours where modern lanes pursue their own paths. The best to follow is perhaps Akeman Street. This ran from St Albans to form the main east–west street of Cirencester. Through most of its length in the Cotswolds it survives as short pieces of minor road. A stretch of its original Roman bank can be seen where it crosses the River Leach, by a footpath through fields a little over one mile to the north of the village of Eastleach Turville. To the south-west of Cirencester its line was continued by a later extension of the original Foss Way, and now forms a modern road (A433) to Kemble Airfield. Beyond the airfield it remains as a footpath along the boundary between Gloucestershire and Wiltshire, on its way to the Roman city of Bath.

The Foss Way zone survived for little more than a decade, for Roman governors were forced by uprisings to press on into North Wales, northern England and, finally, 40 years after the invasion, into Scotland. But the later history of the province indicates the soundness of the initial choice. There were important Roman cities to the north of the Foss – Wroxeter, Chester and York. There are fertile agricultural areas with substantial country houses in the Midlands and the Vale of York. But the bulk of the native tribes, which were politically centralised and were already absorbing civilised Mediterranean practices, lay to the south of the Severn–Trent line, and, in the main, the villas and well-ordered countryside of the Roman period were to be found in this same area. Once across this early zone and into the Pennine foothills, the land, 300 years after the invasion, was still to be dominated by military bases.

Roman towns

The Roman statesman and historian, Tacitus, a contemporary of the British conquest, took a prejudiced view of the process of Romanisation. 'They create a desolation,' he said, 'and call it civilisation.' But Tacitus admired the noble savagery of the northern Barbarians and lamented its passing, and there is little sign that the natives saw the new styles of life in so gloomy a way.

In the Cotswolds the principal town was Cirencester, and a great deal of digging has revealed much of its early history. After the removal of the troops northwards to deal with the natives in Wales, the village which had grown up outside the fort was replanned on the largest scale. The administrative centre with its great hall was the largest civilian complex we know of outside London, and the final size of the town – at about 240 acres some two-thirds that of London – rivalled that of the greatest cities in north-west Europe. Outside the town lay a massive amphitheatre, imposing even in its present ruin.

As was normal, despite its importance, Cirencester was at first without defences, until in the later 2nd century some sense of insecurity (still only dimly understood) prompted the citizens of many Roman towns to begin the long task of enclosing themselves first in earthworks and then in masonry walls. Within, the town was divided into 15 street blocks, some parts of which have now been examined. Here, as in other Roman towns where excavations have revealed a large tract of the urban area, what is remarkable is that luxurious town houses are numerous. We must conclude that the urban population was disproportionately wealthy. Our model of the Romano–British town should not be industrial Birmingham, but Hampstead, Welwyn or Regency Bath. Its inhabitants presumably included a high proportion of the native nobility, not living now in the great wooden roundhouses of their old tradition, but in stone and timber mansions, decorated with painted plaster and mosaic floors.

The country houses

The town houses resembled the most striking feature of the Roman countryside, the villas. A wealthy man would own at least two properties – one in the town, and the other in the country not

far from the city – as the 4th-century writer, Ausonius, said, so that he could pass from one to the other at whim. A recent study of Roman Britain has demonstrated the point: the larger the town, the more numerous were the villas which were scattered within easy reach; the further one goes from a town, with few exceptions, the fewer country houses are to be found.

Cirencester, as befitted its importance, is the centre of a wide band of wealthy villas. Half the known mosaics from Roman Britain are in the south-west, and a very large number of these have been found in the Cotswold villas. Grandest of all is the palatial Woodchester, beside Stroud. The enormous complex extended over more than two acres and centred on an elaborate series of state apartments richly decorated with mosaics, some of which are periodically unearthed for display. Another, well worth a visit, is Chedworth, some six miles north-east of Cirencester, a little smaller than Woodchester but highly ornamented. A particularly fine example, somewhat smaller in scale, has now been opened to view at Great Witcombe near the Ermin Way south of Gloucester.

Even the greatest of the villas was clearly used in part for agriculture. The outer courtyards of Woodchester and Chedworth probably contained barns and similar buildings. In the smaller villas, such as Barnsley Park, the barn stands close to the house and paddocks encroach on the walls of the main building. At the lower end of the scale agricultural need predominated and the building was no more than a substantial farmhouse with few social pretensions.

Away from towns and from rural marketing centres, the rural population continued to have a life-style similar to that of their Iron Age forebears. Important work on the gravels around Lechlade has shown a steady development of a series of Iron Age farmsteads. Some, which

The Four Seasons mosaic pavement, now on display at the Corinium Museum, Cirencester.

developed during a prosperous period, may include a wayside shrine; later ones consist of a small but Romanised farmhouse and outbuildings. The sites, their information salvaged during gravel extraction, are unfortunately not now visible, but they stand as an exemplar by which we can understand the hundreds of small Romano–British native settlements recorded only as marks on aerial photographs. It was by the labour of the inhabitants of innumerable such places that the rich landowners were able to build these massive villas and prominent public buildings, which today survive as a monument to an elaborate, imported way of life.

The end of Roman Britain
From the middle of the 3rd century onwards the Roman Empire passed through civil wars, reconstructions, barbarian incursions, and finally began to fall apart through the great Germanic invasions of the 5th century. There is little sign of these traumatic events in the Cotswolds. In this period Cirencester grew in importance. About AD 300 it was chosen as the capital of one of the provinces into which Britannia was now divided and probably received the governor and his entourage. The local villas prospered, and the 4th century is the great period of elaboration of the Cirencester school of mosaics.

Both Gloucester and Cirencester remained urban centres into the 5th century. Recent work in the centre of Gloucester has shown that the forum, site of the town's administration and market, may have been turned over increasingly to industry and housing, and stone buildings were being erected after AD 370. At Cirencester the forum was being repaired well into the 5th

century. But by now their official function was obsolete, for Britain was independent of the Empire, abandoned as a dispensable outlier of Europe at a time when barbarian Visigoths and Vandals were striking into Gaul and Italy. The new rulers of the province were the local notables, probably ultimately of native origin, who may even have been the far descendants of the Celtic nobles of pre-Roman Britain.

Anglo-Saxon colonists by the middle of the 5th century were occupying parts of eastern England, and Roman patterns there were fast disappearing. No documentation exists for the Cotswolds, but at Withington, six miles south-east of Cheltenham, a strong case has been made for continuity from a Roman villa estate to a medieval village. Other estates near Winchcombe may have developed similarly, and at Frocester near Stroud excavations have demonstrated the conversion of the villa into a complex of timber buildings, presumably a chieftain's residence of this period. The Roman buildings did not always survive – the villas became dilapidated and were abandoned in favour of native houses. The Romano–British were reverting to the pattern of the Celtic, Iron Age past; their town councillors became noblemen, the strongest became hereditary rulers, and the royal palaces may well have been

Coin of Agrippa, Corinium Museum, Cirencester.

set up in the old town halls.

Very little is known of rural settlement in this time of change. Excavations at Crickley Hill have shown a huddle of stone and turf houses tucked behind the ruined rampart of the hill-fort. It seems to have been a small peasant village. But a couple of hundred yards away on the same hilltop a palisaded enclosure contained more substantial buildings, and seems to have been the home of someone altogether more powerful, perhaps a local noble whose ancestors occupied one of the several small villas in the plain beneath the hill. The return to Iron Age patterns is clear, and the towns, their function as centres of civilisation and Roman administration gone, withered away. In Gloucester a layer of black soil, probably from fields, overlay the ruins of the Roman buildings. At Cirencester the amphitheatre outside the walls may have been restored as a strongpoint. Elsewhere the Roman world passes into oblivion, until the first record of the new Anglo-Saxon overlords. At Dyrham near Bath, in 577, Saxons killed three British kings and then captured the three principal towns of the Cotswolds – Bath, Cirencester and Gloucester.

Cotswold Villages

How often have I paused on every charm,
The sheltered cot, the cultivated farm,
The never-failing brook, the busy mill,
The decent church that top the neighbouring hill . . .

Oliver Goldsmith's description of Cotswold villages still rings true 200 years after he penned these lines.

There are few towns on the Cotswold hills; all are country market towns grown up on the Cotswold wool trade – Tewkesbury, Cheltenham, Gloucester and Bath are of the vales. It is, therefore, the 200 or so villages that are the heart of the Cotswolds; a handful trade as towns, others are hardly hamlets – all are woven into the tapestry of the landscape.

Variety in the vernacular

The style in which the Cotsaller built his simple cot to shelter his sheep on the high and rolling wolds (hence the name 'Cotswold'), his humble home, his monastery's tithe barn, his lord's manor and his Maker's church was imposed by purpose rather than by design.

Long before the Roman invasion the local stone was quarried, cut and used for building. The stone lintels, walls and chamber roofs of the Neolithic burial site of Belas Knap on the high plateau above Cleeve Hill are witness to the skill of the early mason and the durability of the stone. The Romans built carefully planned towns in their own distinctive architectural style and enriched their country villas with mosaic pavements of great artistic design, but the walls of their rural estates and the *tesserae* (small stone or clay cubes used in mosaics) of their murals were of Cotswold stone.

The Saxons were farming folk and settled their communities on the hillsides and in the valleys, on wide open wolds and in secret,

wooded combes. Their domestic buildings were mainly of timber and thatch, but most of their churches were of stone. Saxon *long-and-short* work, where broad horizontal stones alternate with narrow vertical ones on the corners of a building, survives in a few churches, as do isolated examples of their carving – crude in comparison with the precision of the Romans and primitive by Norman standards. The church at Daglingworth has fine cable mouldings carved on the doorway, and above it is one of the finest Saxon mass-dials (to indicate the time for mass) in the country. Prudent use has been made of a Roman stone altar – upended and pierced through, it becomes two tiny windows in the vestry wall. Saxons at neighbouring Duntisbourne Rouse used Roman stone coffin lids as seats inside their church porch.

Almost all the villages in the Cotswolds were established by the time of the Norman invasion. Few are not included in the great Domesday census, so most villages can claim Saxon roots.

The conquerors set about their building with vigour, and Gloucestershire is rich in surviving Norman church architecture, but it is the medieval builders who left the Cotswolds their great heritage. They built manor, farm, barn and cottage on a basic design: an essential principle of solid foundations, sturdy walls and roofs steeply pitched to carry the weight of the tilestones.

Cotswold stone itself brings variety to the buildings of the region; the varying degrees of mineral iron in the limestone strata account for differences in the colour of the stone. North wold quarries produced the honey-coloured stone found around Chipping Campden, Broadway and Stanton. Iron-rich rock gives Stanway its burnished gold distinction and is used to such striking effect to face the starkly simple lines of Prinknash Abbey close to Cranham village – quarried at Goscombe it is generally known as Guiting stone. Quarries of the central wolds produce a pearly-white stone; those in the south tend towards a soft grey.

Variations on the basic style evolved as a result of increased prosperity, reflected in size, stature and embellishment. Schools of local masons who knew their native stone, quarried and built with it, mostly to their own designs, raised domestic architecture to become the classic Cotswold style, copied in part or whole over the entire region. Church and barn, manor-house, cottage, pigsty and privy would have come from the same quarry; the same handful of masons would have raised the walls and laid the *slats* (tiles) on the high-pitched roofs, and the village blacksmith would have wrought the hinges, knobs and latches. So each village evolved with its own identity, all of a piece.

Buff-coloured stone houses in Little Rissington on the grassy Cotswold uplands (main picture) contrast with the timber-built style in the rich farmland of the Severn plain (below left).

Placenames

Cotswold placenames are essentially English. With the exception of Gloucester, Cirencester, and Frocester, which keep to their ancient Romano-British roots, the majority are derived from the Anglo-Saxon tongue.

A study of the placenames is fascinating and absorbing. Mainly they are straightforward statements of siting or shape with sometimes an early patron's name appended. Topographical features appear, as in Stow-on-the-Wold and Bourton-on-the-Hill, Wotton-under-Edge and simply Edge along the escarpment, and Winchcombe, Rendcomb and Stinchcombe indicate their positions in a cove-like valley, or combe.

Fords, wells, springs and brooks are indicated in such names as Burford, Fairford, Westwell, Broadwell, Seven Springs, Fulbrook and Swinbrook. Many villages beside a river form groups: twins, triplets and even quadruplets from parent stream or brook are affectionately known as The Ampneys, The Swells, The Colns – like families, and each, like different members of a family, has individual characteristics. Their upstream or downstream position is the usual forename, so Upper Swell and Lower Swell; the ancient form of *nether* for 'lower' retained only in Nether Westcote. Composite names often embody both direction and base, as in Northleach and Eastleach on the River Leach.

Saxon *cot*, variably spelt as *cott* or *cote*, meant 'cottage', giving a clue to that village having grown from smaller roots than one that ends with *ton*, from Saxon *tun* meaning 'farmstead'. Cotswold dialect has given colour and cadence to the basic components and altered many sounds. 'Farmstead by the pool' has been reversed and comes down the centuries as Poulton, pronounced 'polltun'. More difficult to recognise is the River Churn in North Cerney and South Cerney, and *stan* for 'stone', as in Stanton and Stanway, but the most deceptive must be the Shiptons, for they owe nothing to nautical ships and everything to the old Cotsaller's pronunciation of 'sheep'.

The shape of the villages

Three major factors decided the initial siting of the early villages: good water supply, fertile land and strategic defence positions.

Villages fall into two basic types: the manorial village, of either a monastic or a feudal lord, in which the houses are grouped round a nucleus of church, manor and farm, as at Notgrove; and the trade route village, which developed on a straggling street plan, as at Barnsley on the old Welsh Way.

Another distinct feature of the village pattern is the village green. A central grassed area where the community's stock could be herded together was essential in the days of marauding invaders and unenclosed fields. Some were mapped out by the manor as a common pulpit for notices and an open court where villagers could witness the rough justice meted out to their fellows in pillory or stocks. Other greens are an inheritance of ancient common rights where cattle can still graze. A pump, pond, or more anciently a well, served both as watering-place and meeting-place – a practice as old as the Scriptures.

Broadway, the show village of the north Cotswolds, is an example of how an original manorial grouping retains its identity while allowing development to extend along the main street. The green is large; the north side is backed by a line of buildings showing the features typical of fine Cotswold architecture – high gables, stone-tiled roofs, steeply pitched with dormer windows, tall and ornate chimneys. A timber-framed black and white house makes due acknowledgement to its Worcestershire roots and adds interest to the overall scene. The Abbot's Grange on the west side dates back to the early 14th century and is the oldest domestic building in the county. As manorial ties weakened, trade strengthened in the coaching era and the village developed on the broad way stretched out east of the green.

Spa Cottages on the Lower Swell to Stow road. A mineral spring was discovered here in 1807.

Development and decline

Broadway, despite its rapid growth, is still a village, as is Bourton-on-the-Water. Both are rooted in antiquity; both have developed on the tourist trade. Other villages which outgrew their manorial origins obtained the rights to hold a fair and a charter for a market early in their history and a number developed as small market towns.

The wool trade of the Middle Ages gave borough status to some 30 villages of the hill country alone; those that survived the decline of the wool industry did so only if they were well sited on developing traffic routes and formed a trading centre for a rural catchment area.

Close proximity to a larger borough meant the decline of some medieval towns. Blockley, though still busy and adapted to changed economies, never developed on the same lines as its neighbours Moreton-in-Marsh and Stow-on-the-Wold; Guiting Power reverted to a quiet village as Winchcombe grew. Prestbury became an adjunct of Cheltenham, and Churchdown and Whaddon down in the vale were swallowed up in the growth of Gloucester as a city.

In a few isolated cases it was the chance of fate which decided the future of the village. Maugersbury in the north was an established trading centre by the 12th century, but Henry I decreed that a borough should be created close by, where the ancient Cotswold ridgeway met the Roman Foss Way – a prime point on an arterial route. The resulting Stow-on-the-Wold prospered as a town; Maugersbury remained a village.

On the outskirts of the village of Lower Swell on the road to Stow is a cottage with an inscription stating that a chalybeate spring was discovered there in 1807. The neighbouring cottage was built as a spa but was never exploited. If it had been, the development of the north and central Cotswolds would have taken a quite different direction, with a spa town instead of a

A row of cottages at Broadway with their bay and dormer windows and steep gables.

Morris men at Chipping Campden.

tiny Cotswold village – a town averted and a village saved.

Culture and tradition

Deep-rooted tradition is welded into the culture of the Cotswolds. Sadly, the strong dialect is fast disappearing under the influences of newcomers and television; what remains is, therefore, all the more worth preserving. However, more tangible than local idiom is local custom.

The Cotswold calendar is punctuated by events renewing ancient ties to the cycle of seed-time and harvest, the dying of the old season and resurrection of the new. So tightly woven into the pattern of village life are these customs that pagan ritual has been absorbed into the fabric of Church tradition.

The pretty village of Randwick in the Painswick valley is an enclave of ancient custom: early in May is the cheese-rolling round the church and the curious mayor-making ceremony, known as the Randwick Wap.

Whitsuntide – now Spring Bank Holiday – sees the continuance of Robert Dover Games and the Scuttlebrook Wake at Chipping Campden, cheese-rolling down the precipitous Cooper's Hill, and Woolsack Races up Tetbury's steep Gumstool Hill.

Well-dressing is a pretty blessing in the little hill village of Bisley on Ascension Day, and, still in the Stroud valley area, the villagers of Painswick encircle their church hand in hand in the Clipping Ceremony in mid-September.

Christmas-tide brings out the Mummers to re-enact the complex ritualistic fight of good conquering evil, interwoven with primitive fertility rites.

Morris men dance their colourful way through the numerous feasts and festivals, fairs and village fetes, announced to all by the Cotswold Town Criers.

The annual fairs, such as Stow Horse Fair and the 'Mops' originated from the statute and hiring fairs, trading under centuries-old charters. The hiring fairs were the forerunners of the employment exchange where workers offered themselves for hire, each wearing a token of his calling – the carter a twist of horsehair in his hatband, the shepherd a lock of wool on his smock.

Village life today

In a strange way it is the affinity with the past that bodes well for the future of this quiet corner of rural England.

Villages depopulated in Victorian times, as new factories drew depressed communities to work in the developing towns, are fast becoming re-settled. The attractions of the Cotswolds are manifold. The temperate pace of a village is both a novelty and a salve to those subjected to the hurly-burly and pressure of city life, so it is often a haven for the retired or a weekend retreat for young families. While this is understandable, it is also easy to see that too great an influx of newcomers, whether transient or resident, could so quickly destroy the very qualities that attracted them there in the first place. ·

Craftwork has been greatly revived in recent years and helps to continue a tradition as well as to provide work in the locality. The watchful eye of a trust such as the one at Stanway and Guiting Power helps to conserve the best of the past and integrate it successfully with the demands of the present. A village must be a living entity, where villagers care for and about their village, preserving its character created over many generations.

The Cotswold Way

The Cotswold Way offers views of more than the Cotswolds to its walkers. As a scarp path there are views far and wide to the south, west and north, across the vales to hills and mountains beyond. About 100 miles long, it was conceived in the 1950s by the Gloucestershire Branch of the Ramblers' Association. The National Parks and Access to the Countryside Act, 1949, provided for the registration of footpaths and gave government support (and money) for the creation of long-distance footpaths. The Cotswold Way was submitted for consideration but did not achieve recognition (or money) and so was shelved. In the late 1960s Gloucestershire County Council revived the idea by sponsoring the Way as one of its countryside initiatives for European Conservation Year in 1970.

For two years a full-time warden supported by a number of volunteers and rambling clubs researched the detailed route. Formal inauguration in National Footpath Week 1970 took the form of various organisations officially walking a portion each.

The Cotswold Way is essentially a linking together of existing rights of way; it is not the resurrection of an ancient route. Inevitably there are gaps which have to be linked by walking along a road or making a large detour round areas where rights of way do not exist or cannot be negotiated. Although the efforts of dedicated volunteers have been enormously successful in filling these gaps and reducing road walking, eventually there has to be official involvement, particularly for diversions.

Volunteers, notably the Cotswold Voluntary Warden Service and the Ramblers' Association, have put in many hours of work to improve the physical standard of the Way. 'Operation Cotswaymark' started in 1975 to waymark the

entire route. This was no mean task and meant taking on 100 miles of landowners. A mile or two of permission was sometimes easy to achieve when it involved just the agent of a big estate; elsewhere one mile might involve a dozen owners.

Although the Highway Authorities have power to enforce waymarking, it was felt better, for the sake of relationships, to seek permission. Most landowners immediately recognised the value of waymarking. Not only does it give walkers a sense of security to know where they have a right to go, it enables farmers to direct those who have strayed back to the correct route.

The method of waymarking uses the Country-

Long-distance hikers enjoy the view from Crickley Hill.

side Commission system of coloured arrows, thus: yellow for walkers (footpaths); blue for horses, walkers and push-bikes (bridleways). This is a nationally recommended system available for use on footpaths and bridleways throughout the country. In addition a similar arrow in white has been used on roads (including unsurfaced ones), with the Cotswold Way denoted by a white spot near the arrow, to show the continuity of a through route. Other circuits of walks may have a different symbol near the arrow.

Ideally one should say goodbye to the car and walk the route in sequence, staying in local accommodation or in a tent. However, readers may wish to walk a section weekend by weekend, or stay at one or two places. If you go with friends, two cars can make the walk easy. Obviously, one car is parked at the end of the day's selected distance and the other transports the walkers to the start. If you are walking solo, a folding bicycle can be used to cycle from the car parked at the end point to the start. Conceal the bike if possible and lock it ready for collection at the end of the day.

You should be physically fit. You will climb 10,000 feet, though you will never be more than 1,050 feet above sea level. You should be well-

A Voluntary Warden places a yellow arrow to indicate a footpath for walkers. The Cotswold Way is now waymarked for its entire length.

shod in good walking boots giving firm support to the ankles. A sweater may be desirable, particularly if it is windy. It always feels several degrees colder on the hills than it does in the vale or in the sheltered places where you may be staying. Waterproofs are essential at most times of year. With luck, you may only need them for sitting on a mossy bank to eat your sandwiches.

To get the best out of the walk obtain one of the guidebooks currently available. Expect to walk no more than two miles an hour on average. Five or six hours' walking a day gives time to linger and explore. The Way has been walked by youngsters upwards of seven years of age, when the programme starts gently with, say, the first days adjusted to seven miles.

The prevailing wind is from the south-west (up the Bristol Channel and the Severn) and the sun runs to the south. So the Way is now considered as a south-to-north route with sun, wind and rain on your back, opposite to the original concept. Here is a 10-day itinerary starting in Bath.

Day 1 – 10 miles   Bath to Cold Ashton
One can think of the Way as a pilgrimage from the great abbey of Bath to the parish church of St James in Chipping Campden. In olden times pilgrims would put their affairs in order, make their wills and commit themselves to the care of the Almighty before setting off. Fortunately today you should be reasonably safe from highwaymen, hostile natives and bogs to swallow you up. The people you are most likely to meet are those who chose to walk the other way!

From Bath Abbey the Way winds through alleyways, past the Georgian elegance of Queen's Square and the Royal Crescent. The Royal Victoria Park, High Common, Primrose Hill and the northern outskirts of Bath lie before Weston 'village'. A charming church and a parade of old buildings give way to a modern development and then the first real entry into and ascent of the hills.

Glancing back towards Bath from Penn Hill, you take your final leave of the Avon valley from Prospect Stile near the racecourse. Northwards the first of 12 hill-forts is reached (Littledown), before the second golf course and the monument to Sir Bevil Granville, killed in the Civil War battle of Lansdown. Thence the Way winds from what was formerly Somerset into former Gloucestershire and the tranquil Hamswell valley before reaching the A46 and Cold Ashton. Opposite the famous Elizabethan manor, a more recent long-distance footpath, the Limestone Link, reaches the end of its journey from the Mendips.

Day 2 – 11 miles   Cold Ashton to Horton
Pennsylvania and Dyrham Wood precede the descent to a lower level reaching Dyrham village. Dyrham Park (National Trust) is open only from the A46 above. The Way follows the outside of the Park wall. Now with much of the stone removed, one can occasionally look into the deer park through the replacement fence. In 577 on the slopes outside the Park the West Saxons defeated the Britons in battle and drove them westwards towards Wales.

North across the busy A46/M4 junction, the Way diverts into Tormarton, passing from Wessex into Mercia. Although Dodington

House is concealed behind trees, the Way crosses farmland of the estate, the wealth of which was built on West Indian sugar plantations worked by negro slaves.

At Old Sodbury the sudden sound of trains marks the unseen western portal of a two-and-a-half mile tunnel on the London–Wales main line. Little Sodbury hill-fort is above the manor where William Tyndale had an early job before his great work of translating the Bible into English, for which he was burnt at the stake. The day closes by reaching Horton.

Day 3 – 9½ miles   *Horton to Wotton-under-Edge* (*Chipping car park*)

The Way ascends the scarp to Hawkesbury Upton and the Somerset Monument, which you may climb for a view from an extra 120 feet up.

From the windswept heights and into the secluded Kilcott valley, the Way passes out of the modern county of Avon into Gloucestershire just before Alderley. A sunken gulley carries the route above Wortley to emerge with extensive views over Nanny Farmer's Bottom. The Cotswolds are full of bottoms!

Wotton is certainly under the edge of the scarp but still high above the vale. It is a friendly and lively working town.

Day 4 – 8½ miles *Wotton-under-Edge to Dursley* (*May Lane car park*)

A brief exploration of Wotton can precede today's walk before climbing to the Jubilee clump of trees and into the National Trust's Westridge Woods.

The Way skirts Brackenbury Ditches hill-fort before reaching the Tyndale Monument. This tower can be climbed, provided you go down into North Nibley and come back up again with the key.

Again a sense of seclusion accompanies you whilst crossing Waterley Bottom. This is in contrast to the heights of Stinchcombe Hill where the route gives superb views as it follows the edge of the golf course before descending into Dursley.

Day 5 – 11 miles   *Dursley to Standish Woods* (*Cripplegate/Shortwood car park*)

Industrial Dursley gives way to the upland of Cam Long Down. Local legend credits the Devil with creating this strange-shaped hill by emptying the contents of his wheelbarrow. Ask local people why!

The flanks of Uley Bury hill-fort are followed by Coaley Woods which have recently undergone considerable thinning. The intriguing name of Hetty Pegler's Tump describes the prehistoric barrow above. Frocester Hill and Coaley Peak

A panoramic view of Cam Long Down, as seen from Uley Bury.

Picnic Site give fine views of the wide sweeps of the Severn.

To avoid Stroud the Way crosses the River Frome, the Stroudwater canal and the railway west of the town, before the rise to Standish Woods.

Day 6 – 8½ miles *Standish Woods to Cooper's Hill (picnic area car park on A46)*
Haresfield Beacon and its hill-fort start the day before you enter the intimacy of beech woodland. The Siege of Cromwell's Stone seen here refers to the Civil War.

Leaving the scarp, the Way now visits Painswick set on its own promontory within its own valleys. The town deserves exploration as a gem of Cotswold architecture. There are some fine mill buildings associated with the cloth trade along the Painswick Stream (not actually on the Way).

Painswick Common, with its Beacon, lies to the north of the town and hosts another hill-fort, Kimsbury, and another golf course. Beech woodland takes over again as far as Cooper's Hill where the car park lies just below the Way.

Day 7 – 10 miles *Cooper's Hill to Leckhampton Hill (Salterley quarry car park)*
The Way coincides with the nature trail to the maypole and then diverges, taking an easier route than the cheese-rolling slope into Cooper's Hill village, which is on the contour of the hill. Witcombe Woods curve round to Birdlip and the Roman Ermin Way. A new route dedicated over Barrow Wake enables the walker to enjoy the same notable view over the Vale of Gloucester as the motorist in the huge lay-by above.

Crickley Hill Country Park offers woodland and archaeology trails before the Way moves towards Leckhampton Hill.

Day 8 – 11½ miles *Leckhampton Hill to Cleeve Common (quarry car park near golf clubhouse)*
Today the route follows the rim of an amphitheatre of hills above Cheltenham, broken by the valleys of the Lilley Brook and the infant Chelt.

Leckhampton Hill was quarried for stone to build Regency Cheltenham. The Devil's Chimney, just below the Way is a relic of this and has now been repaired to keep it as a notable landmark.

Passing through the gorse onto Charlton Kings Common, the route descends gently to Seven Springs. Strictly off the Way, just round the corner on the A436 Gloucester road, the Springs mark the source of the Churn, which, because it is the remotest source of the Thames and its tributaries, gives rise to claims to be *the* source of the Thames.

Now follows a mile of road walking which it is hoped to change one day. It can be avoided by

North Nibley and the monument to William Tyndale, the translator of the New Testament.

using tracks and paths further 'inland', but this adds an extra mile before rejoining the road before Ravensgate Common. Lineover Wood leads down to Dowdeswell Reservoir, from which the climb leads to open fields and the Happy Valley. This valley runs parallel with the scarp. The view is concealed, creating a secluded feeling before opening out to present Cleeve Common, the highest and the wildest part of the walk.

The hill-fort on the edge, however, boasts a golf course green actually inset in the rampart – to the displeasure of archaeologists. The Way passes through the golf course, with the wilder country being reserved for tomorrow.

Day 9 – 13 miles   *Cleeve Common to Stanton (car park at lower end of village)*

At this stage you should be fit enough to tackle the longest day. In these 13 miles the experience is of the greatest remoteness the Cotswolds can give, contrasted with the bustle of a country town. The eastern part of Cleeve Common is the nearest the Cotswolds come to the wild uplands of the National Parks. Even the farmland beyond gives that delicious excitement of being far from civilisation.

The long barrow of Belas Knap precedes the descent into Winchcombe. At Abbey Terrace the Cotswold Way is joined by the Wychavon Way completing its 40-mile course from Droitwich across the lush Vale of Evesham.

The altarpiece of St Michael's Church, Stanton, much refurnished early this century.

The Pilgrim's Way leads to Hailes Abbey. On the scarp at Beckbury Camp an ornamental seat is provided at Cromwell's Clump (Henry VIII's Thomas Cromwell this time). Legend relates that he witnessed the dismantling of Hailes Abbey from this point, but the trees have grown well in the last 400 years to conceal the view.

The final descent of the day reaches Stanway, with its great house, and leads to an amble across parkland and fields to Stanton.

Day 10 – 10 miles   *Stanton to Chipping Campden*

Stanton is a model of a Cotswold village restored to its present condition by the initiative of one man, Sir Philip Stott. The street carries the Way up the hill and gives a parting glance at the Guildhouse, a modern creation for learning and practising various crafts, built by another inspired individual, Mary Osborne.

The scarp walk continues with wide views on the way to Broadway in Worcestershire. Broadway draws the crowds. One can understand why and appreciate it despite them.

The climb to Broadway Tower is the last as the journey closes with a final sweep of the wolds before dropping down into the beauty of Chipping Campden.

The official end of the Way is by the Market Hall, but you may care to go a little further to St James's Church and give thanks for a safe arrival as requested in that prayer at Bath Abbey!

Guide books on The Way are available in bookshops, and for further information on accommodation contact: Cotswold Warden Office, County Planning Department, Shire Hall, Gloucester, GI1 2TN.

Stone-built houses overgrown with climbers at the delightful village of Stanton, sensitively restored by Sir Philip Stott.

COTSWOLDS
Gazetteer

AT THE
HOP POLE, *Tewkesbury*
*They stopped to dine upon which
occasion there was more Bottled Ale,
with some more Madeira and some
Port besides and here the Case Bottle
was replenished for the fourth time.
Under the influence of these combined
stimulants Mr. Pickwick & Mr. Ben Allen
fell fast asleep for thirty miles
while Bob & Mr. Weller sang
duets in the dickey.*

PICKWICK PAPERS, Chap. 50.

*Each entry in this Gazetteer has the atlas
page number on which the place can be
found and/or its National Grid reference
included under the heading. An
explanation of how to use the National
Grid is given on page 76.*

*Above: Plaque on the Royal Hop Pole Hotel, Tewkesbury,
which extended its hospitality to Mr Pickwick.*

The church at Ampney St Mary now stands isolated from its community, which, destroyed by the Black Death, was rebuilt about half a mile away.

The Ampneys

Map Ref: 94SP0801

Ampney brook never achieved the status of a river but has given its name to an area far beyond its headwaters. Ampney Down marks its northerly point as it touches the Roman Foss Way (A429), on the Cirencester to Stow road, with Ampney Sheephouse close to the Welsh Way where the old drovers took their herds on the hoof westward to Gloucester markets.

Ampney Crucis is the largest of the three Ampneys on the Cirencester to Fairford road. A turning off the main road by the Crown of Crucis inn leads over a bridge to a picturesque corner of old millhouse, minute village green, a trim little lodge house and an evergreen bower through which the ancient church is located. The fine churchyard cross and Holy Rood dedication of the cruciform church accounts for the Crucis.

Ampney St Peter, compactly grouped on a single street off the main road, has great charm in its simple style. Across the road to the south-east is Ranbury Ring, a Neolithic encampment. ·

The third of the Ampneys was wiped off the banks of the little brook by the Black Death. Ampney St Mary was rebuilt at Ashbrook, the 'east brook', really a stream tributary of the Ampney brook, some half a mile away to the north. Only the little church remains in a field alongside the main road. Locally called the Ivy Church from the days when it stood in ivy-clad neglect, it is back in service today attracting attention to its medieval wall-paintings and bold Norman tympanum depicting a graphic moral of good conquering evil. It is an isolated, tranquil spot where only the sound of the brook breaks the silence as it goes on to complete the quartet with Down Ampney, some four miles away to the south.

Ampney St Mary Church, known locally as the Ivy Church, has some interesting medieval wall paintings.

Badminton

Map Ref: 78ST8082

Badminton is now synonymous with the grace and rigour of the famous three-day event held each April, a mecca for horse-loving folk to thrill at the supreme skills of top-class riders in the company of the Royal Family.

The seat of the Dukes of Beaufort for some three centuries, Badminton was laid out on the most ambitious landscaping plan of all the Gloucestershire great estates. On the Tetbury to Bath road it is bounded by a five-mile avenue of glorious beech trees, and the lodges at the ends of the drives are distinguished by castellated turrets and towers.

Great Badminton is a perfect example of an estate village; the almshouses bear the ducal arms and the broad street is trim and neat.

The parish church of St Michael is attached to the mansion house and furnished with classical monuments and exquisite sculptures of the Beaufort family. The most elaborate, to the first Duke who died in 1699, was brought from the Beaufort Chapel at Windsor and necessitated the building of the chancel at Badminton to accommodate it.

Paradoxically, it is the small Cotswold stone-tiled church at neighbouring Little Badminton which is the private ducal chapel. Thatched cottages and farm buildings cluster round the village green, a circular dovecote being its focal point.

AA recommends:
Guesthouse: Moda Hotel,
I High Street, Chipping Sodbury,
tel. Chipping Sodbury 312135
Garage: TT Motors, Hatters Lane,
Chipping Sodbury, *tel.* Chipping Sodbury
313181

The Barringtons

Map Ref: 91SP2013

Viewed from the high ridge road of the A40, Little Barrington settles like a toy in the broad valley below – the Windrush winking as it catches the noonday sun. The road descends between high shrubby banks and the little village opens out at the bottom.

Cottages cluster on raised paths around the village green as on the rim of a bowl, the humpy hollow providing the stone for their building. A trickle of a stream in the bottom keeps it green with tall wetland plants.

Cottages at Little Barrington. Barrington stone was much in demand by architects like Sir Christopher Wren.

The church stands apart, on a side road. There is much Norman masonry in this mainly 14th-century building, including a clear cut tympanum on the north wall.

The road sweeps round the green and winds over the river. The Fox on the corner is the only pub for some half-a-dozen of the valley villages.

The Barringtons are synonymous with stone. Little Barrington was the home of the notable Strong family whose work under Christopher Wren took both mason and stone from this quiet Cotswold corner to rebuild some of the finest of London's buildings after the Great Fire.

The short stretch of road between the two low bridges is still known as Strong's Causeway after Thomas Strong, who laid the foundation stone of St Paul's Cathedral. Thomas left money to 'make a way between the Barrington bridges . . . to carry a corpse in safety'.

Great Barrington is an estate village. A very high wall encloses the park, its Palladian mansion of which Pope wrote 'at Barrington shall English Bounty stand', and the parish church. The village goes eastward alongside the road with farms behind and on to Taynton and Burford, across the flat mead through which the Windrush meanders.

Medieval Legacy

If you stand in the market-place of a small Cotswold town like North-leach, surrounded by worn stone houses and dominated by its enormous church, or if you walk down the steep hill of Burford with ancient buildings crowding in around, then you may well have a strong impression of an unchanging medieval past. The reality is very different, for the old stone villages and small towns that dot the Cotswold landscape owe most of their form to the massive rebuilding that spread through the area after the 15th century.

In the early Middle Ages the landscape probably looked little different from its prehistoric pattern of dispersed farms and hamlets. The traveller through Saxon England would find some differences, of course. Churches would be the most obvious novelty, but for a long period there were only a few — monastic establishments in Gloucester, Cirencester, Tewkesbury, Winch-combe and Deerhurst. The parish churches which now form such notable landmarks belong to the replanning of the land which was going on in the last century or two before the Norman Conquest.

By 1250 at least 20 new boroughs had been founded in the area. Many, like Moreton-in-Marsh, Northleach, or Chipping Campden clearly had a small old centre to which was now attached a grid of new streets. We know a little about these places from excavations. Houses were at first single-storeyed, built largely of timber with stone foundations; streets were roughly cobbled, and the backyards were choked with rubbish pits.

Changes began in the later 13th century. With increasing prosperity because of the expanding woollen industry we find heavy investment in buildings. The most striking are the barns built by the major landlords to house their crops. Among the oldest, and as large as almost any in England, is Great Coxwell near Faringdon, Oxfordshire. A similar monastic barn, at the other end of our region, is Bredon near Tewkesbury, now restored after a terrible fire in 1980. Both are well worth a visit, and the comparison between these magnificent structures and those rude peasant houses found in excavations underlines the vast gulf in medieval society between the rich and the poor.

Even prosperous houses were still built largely of wood. When we look at the medieval houses of Burford, all we can see on the street side is honey-yellow Cotswold stone. A survey of these buildings, however, has revealed that the stonework is a late facade applied towards the end of the Middle Ages. Behind the fronts stand the remains of timber-framed houses, improved and brought up to date by new fashions.

These fashions have left a permanent mark on the Cotswolds. Steep stone roofs, a profusion of gabled dormer windows, doorways decorated with flat pointed heads, and the characteristic rectangular drip-mouldings around the windows. Take a picture of a Cotswold scene, and its buildings will immediately identify it. This is the impression that the visitor will take away from the Cotswolds, a land of broad rolling fields and pasture, of narrow wooded valleys, of small stone village and winding roads thick with hedges, wonderful in May.

The interior of the early 14th-century barn at Great Coxwell, near Faringdon, Oxfordshire.

Bath

Map Ref: ST7464

Roman grandeur and Georgian grace fuse into exuberance at Bath.

It was *aquae sulis* – the waters of the sun – which gave Bath both its name and fame. For here at the southernmost tip of the Cotswolds the Romans discovered hot springs of constant temperature and output unique in Britain.

Easily won from the hills and soft enough to work when freshly quarried, but rock-like on exposure, the Cotswold stone was ideal for building an impressive town around the hot-water springs. Of the houses, temples and baths which served the Romans for 400 years, the Great Bath with the Abbey towering majestically behind it is the most memorable.

Magnificent as the Abbey is, the Norman Cathedral it replaced was on an even grander scale.

The Saxons had crowned the first King of all England in an even older church. The west front of the Gothic Abbey is an extravaganza of figures and features and filigree finely carved – breathtakingly beautiful in its entirety.

The town was involved in the medieval wool trade, but the attraction of the hot springs brought it more prosperity and publicity. By Tudor times the state of the baths and the junketings of the bathers brought caustic comment and action from the corporation. Elizabeth I visited in 1574 and the waters were said by physicians to have medicinal qualities.

A succession of royal visits made it a fashionable spa resort to which the sociables and notables of the day came to promenade their finery, wine and dine to excess and ameliorate their ailments by 'taking the waters'.

Despite a regular royal patronage, Bath owes its distinction to the flamboyant dictator Richard (Beau) Nash, who under his honorary title of Master of Ceremonies ruled the social scene for 50 years; the financial backing of Ralph Allen, who promoted the use of the creamy local limestone; and the architectural genius of John Wood. Georgian buildings sweep through Bath in stunning symmetry.

Excavations of the Roman town continue to fill the excellent museum, but there is plenty to keep today's visitor interested in festivals and numerous events which are staged somewhere within Bath's flower-filled city streets.

AA recommends:
Hotels: Royal Crescent, 16 Royal Crescent, 4-star, *tel.* 319090
Priory, Weston Road, 1-rosette, 3 red star, *tel.* 331922
Self Catering: Flats 2, 3 & 4,
1 Grosvenor Place, *tel.* Malmesbury 2612
Marshal Wade's House, 14 Abbey

The Roman Bath with the 15th-century Abbey Church behind, at Bath.

Churchyard, *tel.* Littlewick Green 5925
Guesthouses: For a large selection of guesthouses see the AA *Guesthouses, Farmhouses & Inns in Britain* guide.
Garages: D & H Motorcycles, 11 Green Park Mews, Midland Bridge, *tel.* 331318
Hinton, Albion Place, Upper Bristol Road, *tel.* 22131 (day), Saltford 2641 (night)
A Richardson & Sons, Bathwick Hill, *tel.* 66286

Berkeley Castle

Map Ref: 78ST6899

Like a faded rose on a lawn, Berkeley Castle's pink-toned walls are now aged and grey against the green of the vale kept lush from the waters of the Little Avon and the strong Severn.

Twelfth-century Berkeley Castle.

Berkeley Castle is one of England's most imposing feudal strongholds and one of the oldest, if not *the* oldest, inhabited homes in Gloucestershire. The earliest part, which survives from the time of Henry II, is the massive stone keep, containing a great hall, a chapel and the dungeon where the ill-fated Edward II was murdered so gruesomely. It forms part of the castle open to the public by the Berkeley family whose home it has been for over 800 years.

Within the magnificent castle's shadow, of humbler proportions but of world-wide importance is the little Temple of Vaccinia. No more than a thatched garden shed with bark plastered on its brick walls, this is where Jenner inoculated his first patients.

Edward Jenner was born in the old vicarage. As a successful medical man he returned to his native Berkeley, pursuing his interests in natural history and music, and his burning ambition to eradicate smallpox which, it had been estimated, caused the deaths of some 60 million victims in the 17th century. The local lad who trustingly submitted himself for Jenner's experimental inoculations was rewarded by the grateful doctor with a cottage for life which, until recently, housed the wealth of Jenner memorabilia. As a result of an appeal and a generous benefaction, the collection has now moved into The Chantry, the doctor's childhood home.

AA recommends:
Hotel: Old Schoolhouse, Berkeley Hotel, Canonbury Street, 2-star, *tel.* Dursley 811711
Guesthouse: Greenacres, Breadstone (2m E off A38) (farmhouse), *tel.* Dursley 810348
Garage: Taylers of Woodford, Woodford (A38), *tel.* Falfield 260133

Bibury

Map Ref: 94SP1106

'The most beautiful village in England' was how William Morris described Bibury. Throughout history people have been drawn to this lovely spot in the central Cotswolds where the hills fold gently down to the Coln valley. Remnants of Celtic fields, an Iron Age hill-fort, a long barrow and beehive chamber with stone cupboards or niches are evidence of early settlement in the area.

The village itself centres on fine old cottages round a square on the north-west side of the church and must be sought out by a detour off the main road. St Mary's is rich in Saxon work and was held as a 'peculiar' by Oxfordshire's Osney Abbey until the Dissolution. The fine collection of sheep corbels pays tribute to the major part that wool once played in the life of the village.

In the same corner is Bibury Court, noble, gabled, and now a hotel, prettily sited on the banks of the Coln as it winds its way out of the village.

The river is a prominent feature of Bibury with the main road running alongside it. The low wall is usually overhung with visitors peering down between the trailing weeds to catch a glimpse of the trout for which the Coln is famous, or amused at the antics of the wildfowl skimming and skidding and skiing the water. Cottages in local style stand back from the road in well-kept gardens.

Across the river is Arlington Row. Backed by dark woods, the tiny cottages which once housed the village weavers are enchanting with their steep-pitched roofs and irregular forms touched with the patina of three centuries. The National Trust owns them and Rack Isle, the water-meadow on to which they face. This takes its name from the time when it was a drying ground for cloth woven in the cottages and fulled at the mill opposite. Awkward Hill in the corner is steeply banked with more attractive cottages.

The Swan Hotel has long been famous as a fisherman's haunt and even earlier as a favourite rendezvous of the gay blades who flocked here for the Bibury Races of King Charles's day. The tiny windowless building close by was the old village lock-up.

Across the bridge is the trout farm and Arlington Mill – now a folk museum. The hamlet of Arlington, concentrated around its green high on a bank, joins with Bibury as the A433 angles off westward to Barnsley and Cirencester.

The minor road by the Swan Hotel follows the upstream course of the Coln valley. Ablington, the nearby hamlet, was the home of Arthur Gibbs, the young squire who

The River Coln flows idly past Arlington Row, a group of 17th-century weavers' cottages now owned by the National Trust.

immortalised it in *A Cotswold Village*, the first of the classics to look at country life with poetic insight.

Winson, up-river, also achieved literary notice as the home of Robert Henriques, author of *Through the Valley*. In a thatched cottage in a corner of the pretty little village is the smallest post office in the West Country.

AA recommends:
Hotels: Swan, 3-star, *tel.* 204
Bibury Court, 2-star Country House Hotel, *tel.* 337

Blockley

Map Ref: 84SP1634

An administrative island of Worcestershire for 1000 years, Blockley was transferred to Gloucestershire in 1931 when many county anomalies were ironed out.

A large village, equidistant from Moreton-in-Marsh and Chipping Campden but not distant enough to develop into a market town itself, Blockley harnessed the water power of the deeply cleft valley early in its history.

Industrialised – albeit on a small scale by modern-day standards – and insular, Blockley has more of the Stroud valley character in its old mills terraced amidst the long rows of cottages along the steep and narrow ledges above the valley, than that of the north wolds village. But the golden glow of local ashlar stone and its architecture establishes its correct geographical identity.

Cheap labour in the aftermath of the agricultural and cloth-trade depressions, and spring-studded hillsides made Blockley a prime choice for the silk-throwing mills based on the Coventry ribbon trade. A hundred years ago six mills employed some 600 people. The buildings have now been converted to other uses, but harmonise well with contemporary cottages and add character to an attractive village.

An attractive corner of Blockley.

Blockley's former stature can be gauged by its church, which was large in Norman times, the busy High Street and the fine manors of Northwick Park and Upton Wold to the north and west. Blockley survived where others could not, for across and under the fields lie two deserted villages – Upton and Middle Ditchford.

AA recommends:
Self Catering: The Cottage, 4 Malvern House, *tel.* 700354
Lower Farm Cottages, *tel.* 700237
Flats 1 & 2, Malvern House, *tel.* 700354
Mill Row Cottages, *tel.* 700678
4 Northwick Terrace, *tel.* 700354
Old Mill Dene, School Lane, *tel.* 01-977-2502
Garage: Stuart Turner, *tel.* 700306

Bourton-on-the-Hill

Map Ref: 84SP1732

An artist's delight is the steep street lined with cottages set prettily in terraced gardens, leading up to the lovely old church on the hill.

The rigours of the rise have been known to travellers from early times and Bourton on its hill was part of the turnpiked 'Great Road' from London and Oxford to Worcester. The modern A44 links this delightful little village readily to the busy centres of Moreton-in-Marsh and Broadway.

As with many small village churches, St Lawrence holds a treasure of the past safely within its ancient walls. Architectural features of 900 years are to be traced in its pillars and carving, its glass and font, its plate and monuments. The Winchester Bushel and Peck, made of bell metal and inscribed with the name of the Magistrate's Clerk, is of special interest. Dating from the time of Elizabeth I the weights and measures of the Winchester Standard – of such accuracy that they set the standard for the whole kingdom – were used to settle disputes relating to the collection of corn tithes.

One of the Cotswolds' finest and largest barns belongs to Bourton House at the east end at the foot of the hill. The rolling downs around the village have been used for horse-training for some 150 years and many national race winners have come from the stables in the area.

AA recommends:
Self Catering: The Gable, *tel.* Hook Norton 737496

Well-kept gardens enhance a row of terraced cottages at Bourton-on-the-Hill.

Bourton-on-the-Water

Map Ref: 90SP1620

Bourton-on-the-Water caters for visitors on a grand scale. Housed in an old watermill is a motor museum with one of the country's largest collections of vintage advertising signs. Exotic butterflies and model railways are on permanent exhibition in the High Street, fish can be viewed at the Trout Farm, and perfume is made in the village.

Flamingoes grace the lawn in front of Chardwar Manor, part of Birdland Zoo Garden at Bourton-on-the-Water.

So long established now as to form part of the village fabric are the Model Village and Birdland, both created by local men with great skill, both acclaimed the best of their kind in the world. The model, an exact replica of the village scaled down to one-ninth the size of the original, is built of Cotswold stone in the garden of the Old New Inn.

Birdland is really a garden of birds, created by the late Len Hill, who was accorded the title 'Penguin Millionaire' when he bought two of the Falkland islands simply to conserve their population of about one million penguins. Some 600 different species of birds from all over the world fill the three-acre garden of Chardwar Manor, the mellowed Tudor house which provides a dignified backdrop to the bright-pink flamingoes ballet-stepping across the lawns, and a fitting home for the distinguished Flight-Lieutenant Frederick, the pelican mascot of the RAF Red Arrows aerobatic flying team.

The river, enhanced by attractive low bridges, is the outstanding natural feature of the village, earning it the label 'the little Venice of the Cotswolds'.

There was a bridge at Bourton in Roman times – a stone plaque on Bourton Bridge shows the badge of the Second Legion who laid out the Foss Way, which crosses the Windrush in a lovely valley of farmland where villagers have settled since the Iron Age. It would be hard to imagine any settlement so perfectly in harmony with its environment as this Cotswold stone-built village of today. Within easy reach are a dozen quiet villages, rare breeds of fowl at Folly Farm and the well-marked footpath route across the dip-slope wolds of the Oxfordshire Way.

AA recommends:
Self Catering: Greenmore, Rectory Lane, *tel.* Cirencester 713295
Porch Cottage, Clapton Row, *tel.* Cotswold 20813
South Lawn Cottage, South Lawn, Victoria Street, *tel.* Cotswold 20813
4 & 5 Victoria Terrace, *tel.* Cotswold 20813
Guesthouse: Mousetrap (inn), *tel.* Cotswold 20579

Bredon and its Hill Villages

Map Ref: 80SO9236

A ring of villages encircles Bredon Hill as pretty as flowers in a garland. Vale-thatched Cotswold stone, timber and brick line the village streets and mix happily in cottage gardens.

Bredon to the south beckons with a slender church spire to its mainly one-street village of black and white, warm red brick and honey-coloured stone, a church with Norman work, mellowed houses of Elizabeth I's day, one of the largest tithe barns in England, and two of its oldest inns.

The low-lying river floods the Ham meadows in winter conserving the natural habitat for its flora and fauna, which together with the old village characters are immortalised in John Moore's *Brensham Village*, his name for Bredon.

The pretty hamlet of Bredon's

The Cotswold Voluntary Warden Service

The Cotswold Voluntary Warden Service was set up in 1968, two years after 582 square miles of the Cotswolds were designated an Area of Outstanding Natural Beauty. Today there is one full-time warden who is responsible for the work carried out by over 200 voluntary wardens, of all ages, recruited from all walks of life, who give their time and services free.

The wardens are always ready to help visitors with guidance and information when they meet on their regular patrols of footpaths, country parks and picnic sites. You will recognise them by their green and yellow armband or badge. They organise a regular series of guided walks including a number of specialised village walks. For the visitor who wishes to walk at his own speed they prepare and publish a series of walks leaflets (list and guided walks programme available from the address below).

Wardens help to make walking in the Cotswolds even more enjoyable by regular patrols of the more popular footpaths (with the Cotswold Way as number one priority) to pin-point problems at an early stage. They then organise work parties to sort out difficulties by clearance work, by waymarking, or by building a stile or set of steps.

With the agreement and co-operation of landowners, wardens help to increase the beauty of areas to which the public have access by planting trees, by laying hedges, and by renewing and maintaining significant drystone walls. They occasionally clear scrubland in order to maintain an important wildlife habitat.

Wardens don't enjoy having to clear up litter which thoughtless people have left behind or deliberately dumped, but they do it! They will carry out litter clearance at a popular site to nip the problem in the bud before a major eyesore develops.

There are a number of experienced wardens who are willing to give illustrated talks about the Cotswolds and the Warden Service and who are trained to show related audio-visual programmes.

Voluntary wardens planting trees at Cooley Peak Picnic Site.

Wardens will help young people on the Duke of Edinburgh's Award Scheme by training them and involving them in practical work.

If you would like to know more about the Voluntary Warden Service or feel they might be able to help you in some way, write to:

Cotswold Warden Office,
c/o County Planning Department,
Gloucestershire County Council,
Shire Hall,
Gloucester GL1 2TN
or telephone: Gloucester 425674.

Norton sheltering under the hill faces the Avon and the distant Malverns. 'Oh, pastoral heart of England' wrote Sir Arthur Quiller-Couch of Eckington Bridge. Despite its narrow width and long years the bridge has stood the test of time and 20th-century transport. Eckington is fruit-and-veg country, the coming of the Gloucester-to-Birmingham railway bringing its markets nearer in the mid-19th century.

The Combertons, Great and Little, pretty in all seasons, are a delight in apple-blossom time.

Two miles away arcing round the hill is Elmley Castle, a picture of black-and-white buildings brought alive by the singing of children dancing round the maypole on Oak Apple Day (29th May). The escape of the fugitive Charles I is kept fresh in the speech of local folk who call the way out of the village 'the hole in-the wall'. This leads to Kersoe and on to Ashton-under-Hill, where farms abutting the streets once provided the living for the village.

There is still 'peace at Grafton' such as John Drinkwater knew. No new building since Victoria's day spoils the village of which the poet wrote, gathering folk songs in Beckford Inn and inspiration from the countryside.

The circle is completed through pretty little Conderton, visited by Joseph Arch to promote his Agricultural Workers' Union; along to parkland Overbury, visited by John Wesley for overnight stabling for his horse and a bed for himself at the Court; and so to the long village of Kemerton. The latter can boast at least two famous residents: the 18th-century squire who built Parson's Folly on top of the hill to make it an even more prominent landmark, and the 20th-century writer, John Moore, who left the literary world the richer through his books about the hill villages of Bredon.

AA recommends:
Self Catering: St Michael's, tel. 73110

Bredon Hill from near Kemerton.

Broadway Tower Country Park

Map Ref: 83SP1136

Almost as a punctuation mark on the north-westerly tip of the Cotswold escarpment, stands the Norman-style, battlemented dark tower on Broadway Beacon.

James Wyatt designed Broadway Tower in the late 18th century for the Sixth Earl of Coventry. He

Broadway

Map Ref: 83SP0937

William Morris, is said to have discovered Broadway and it is easy to see how he was captivated by this village of corn-coloured stone lying just off the scarpline on the rich soil of Worcestershire.

As English as apple pie, Broadway has remained as unchanged as is possible under the pressures of tourism, for it is a virtual honey-pot of visitors, and the village caters for them accordingly.

A bevy of artists followed in the wake of William Morris – his friend, Frank Millet, lived at Farnham House and died in the great Titanic disaster; J M Barrie, Vaughan Williams and Elgar – all drew inspiration from the line and form, texture and composition of what was then the typical English village.

The oldest of its two churches lies about a mile to the south of the village centre, on the Snowshill road. St Eadburgh's had served the villagers for seven centuries before the Victorians decided it was too much of a trek and built St Michael's close to the village green. The 14th-century Grange and the Crown and Trumpet pub add interest in different forms to the corner.

The 'broad way' is the main street, lined with red chestnut trees. Situated on the main route between Oxford and Worcester, the village developed because of the stage-coach trade. Both King Charles and Oliver Cromwell stayed here at different times.

Of the many beautiful buildings it is the Lygon Arms (pronounced 'Liggon') that is the most striking. The success of the village as a staging-post really stems from the business acumen of General Lygon's butler who foresaw great

Above left: Broadway Tower, now the central feature of the Country Park, commands, on a clear day, a view of 12 counties.
Above right: View from the Tower window.

potential in what was then the White Hart Inn. The butler bought the inn from his master – who was more preoccupied with planting his parkland at Springhill above the village with beech trees in Waterloo Battle formation – and named it the Lygon Arms. Some two dozen inns opened up around the same time, and Broadway prospered since fresh and extra horses were in demand for the steep haul up the long Fish Hill on the A44 leading out of the village. The quaintly-styled Fish Inn stands at the top of the serpentine hill.

Fish Hill picnic site on the north side of the inn is a free area of 12 acres of grass and woodland with a nature trail, open all the year. A topograph puts names to the superb views; it is probably the only self-draining topograph in the country – for rain falling on the deeply incised Severn flows away! Over the road is the Broadway Tower Country Park.

AA recommends:

Hotels: Lygon Arms, 4 red star, *tel.* 852255
Dormy House, Willersley Hill (2m E off A44 in Gloucestershire), 3-star, *tel.* 852711
Collin House, Collin Lane, 2-star Country House Hotel, *tel.* 858354
Self Catering: Bibsworth Lodge, *tel.* Cirencester 713295
Charity Cottage, Charity Farm, Stanton, *tel.* Stanton 339
Oak Hill Farm Holidays, Snowshill, *tel.* 858758
The Old Music Room, *tel.* Fairford 713295
Guesthouses: Old Rectory, Church Street, Willersey, *tel.* Evesham 853729
Olive Branch, 78-80 High Street, *tel.* 853440

followed the fashion for follies as part of the landscaping of the estate by Capability Brown, yet chose a darker stone than the native Cotswold in order to create an appearance of brooding maturity.

At 1,024 feet, the second highest point on the Cotswolds, the 65ft tower dominates the skyline above the village of Broadway and commands a panoramic view over a dozen counties; the keen-sighted can identify the distinctive lines of Warwick Castle, Worcester Cathedral and Tewkesbury Abbey. A telescope on the roof extends the range of vision on a clear day to scan from the countryside of the Midlands to the Welsh mountains, and a relief map on the third floor puts the landmarks into perspective.

William Morris, a frequent visitor, who wrote a letter from the Tower in 1876 which spearheaded the formation of the Society for the Protection of Ancient Buildings, is duly accorded a permanent exhibition on the second floor, and the eccentric bibliophile, Sir Thomas Phillips, who set up the Middle Hill Press in the Tower, is remembered by a printing press on the ground floor which visitors can use.

Education and recreation happily merge: the Tower Barn is a typical Cotswold stone-built and tiled barn some 150 years old; a small model illustrates the age-old craft of Cotswold stone *slatting*, demonstrating how some 18,000 slates were used to roof the barn. An adventure playground, containing England's only whirligig, a collection of birds and farm animals, a giant chess game and refreshment facilities are close by the tower.

Nature trails lead through woodland and to Fish Inn on the busy A44, and follow, albeit briefly, the road where Roman legions once marched across the Cotswolds.

Burford

Map Ref: 91SP2512

This is the stone country of the Cotswolds; from the quarries on the eastern edge came the easily worked oolite limestone to rebuild many of London's churches after the Great Fire, St Paul's Cathedral, Blenheim Palace, Oxford's colleges and the Sheldonian Theatre – and Burford.

Approached off the A40 at the roundabout, Burford's long main street descends steeply down the hill in Lilliputian scale against a backcloth of softly moulded wold and water-meadow. Grey-gabled houses with lichen-encrusted roofs, shops and tearooms, haughty-height hotels and comforting old inns line the street; a jumbled juxtaposition of home and trading post, resident and tourist sleeping together under a roof ridge crookedly sloped against the skyline. A line of limes in a wide grass verge separates the buildings from the road down to the memorial cross.

The Tolsey, a market house of Tudor date, now housing the museum, holds out its great round clock as though to remind visitors to take time to explore the by-streets and back-lanes of this old grey town. The ancient Priory, now a closed nunnery, lies to the west, holding the memories of 'pretty witty Nell' and her merry monarch within its austere walls. Their son born in 1670 was created Earl of Burford and Nell Gwyn named her rooms at Windsor Burford House.

It was the famous races across the seven downs to the south-west that brought royalty and riff-raff, gentlefolk and gamblers to cram the town. This great sporting event, that lasted over 200 years, declined with the enclosure of the open fields, but the new coaching era boosted the town economy and left fine old

The steep wide main street at Burford.

hostelries in its wake.

The church with its splendid spire stands to the east at the foot of the hill in a pocket of history. A Royalist captive left the word 'prisner' and the date scratched inside the font; Warwick 'the Kingmaker' left a legacy of fine old almshouses, and Symon Wysdom, an alderman, founded the first school here in 1577.

The northerly point of the town terminates at the low stone bridge; across the river is countryside. On the high road to the south is a wildlife park, with ample facilities for visitors, where animals from all over the world roam in acres of parkland.

AA recommends:
Self Catering: The Mill at Burford, *tel.* 2379
Widford Farm Cottages, *tel.* 2152
Guesthouse: Corner House Hotel, High Street, *tel.* 3151

Castle Combe

Map Ref: 78ST8477

As the great Foss Way reaches down to the south-west out of Gloucestershire and into the rich farm- and parklands of the south wolds, this delightful little village appears as a honey-coloured stone oasis, settled as it is in the hollow of a deeply wooded combe.

It has the spirit of King Alfred's Wessex in its composition, though the pinnacled tower amid the trees is of church not castle. The castle which gave the combe its name has long since vanished. Sir Walter, who built it, has slept the sleep of seven centuries in St Andrew's which was founded by the wealthy clothiers of the district.

The wool trade of the Middle Ages left a fine old market cross atop stone steps, mellowed and hollowed with the wear of 500 years. It stands at the top of the street where the pretty porched cottages closely face their neighbours. A three-arched bridge of rough-hewn stone spans the little Bybrook at the bottom in front of a corner of cottages.

Parking is restricted to the edge of the village which keeps this lovely spot clear of the clutter of cars. Castle Combe has survived the tourists that flock to see it and has even emerged unspoiled after assuming the guise of a seaport in the film set for *Doctor Doolittle*.

AA recommends:
Hotel: Manor House, 3-star, Country House Hotel, *tel.* 782206
Garage: Circuit Motors, *tel.* 782596

Castle Combe, one of the most beautiful villages in England.

Chedworth

Map Ref: 88SP0511

Settled amid a patchwork of fields is
Chedworth – its stone-built
cottages scattered among pretty
gardens on the steep hillsides
bounding the Coln Valley.

Fine old cottages of the mid-18th
century radiate from a church with
Norman foundations and a manor-
house with medieval origins,
grouped on the typical English
village plan. Steep-pitched gables
and mullioned windows typify the
Cotswold style in large and small
houses alike, and the visit of
Elizabeth of York 500 years ago is
perpetuated in Queen Street.

Keeping faith with the self-
sufficient living once imposed on
such isolated communities,
Chedworth still attracts artists and
craftsmen and retains the character
of a living village, not just a
weekenders' haunt.

Above the village at Denfurlong a
farm trail is open all the year
allowing an insight into modern
dairy and arable farming.

Sheltered in a beautiful combe,
Chedworth Roman Villa was
discovered in 1864 by a
gamekeeper, who noticed that
rabbits burrowing in the woods
were throwing up loose *tesserae*. The
mosaic floors are fine examples of
the craft practised some 1500 years
ago. Particularly beautiful is the one
in the west wing where figures
depicting the four seasons are

*Detail from the Four Seasons mosaic
floor at Chedworth showing the figure
depicting Summer.*

shown in each corner. Fascinating
finds and plans of the site are
displayed in the adjacent museum
which, together with the villa, is
owned by the National Trust.

AA recommends:
Garage: Clifford & Webb, Old Brewery
Yard, Northleach, *tel.* Northleach 306

Cheltenham Spa

Map Ref: 87SO9422

'Pretty, poor and proud' –
Cheltenham has attracted more
elegant titles over the years, but a
local maxim is always worth looking
at in detail.

Cheltenham spreads along a
terrace under the great bluff of
Cleeve Hill, the highest point of the
Cotswolds and above the flat vale
lands watered by the Severn.

It is pretty. The Promenade has
been described as the most
beautiful thoroughfare in Britain. It
is outstanding in its composition of
elegant Regency buildings
separated from the main road by
wide flower-bedded greens and an
avenue of trees, with high-class
shops and boutiques making a
bustling contrast on the opposite
side.

There is no evidence of poverty
in Cheltenham today – rather it is
smart, fashionable and prosperous.
Tourists are attracted to it for its
style, its art gallery and museum,
Holst's birthplace, its theatre and
the international festivals of music
and literature, the famous
Cheltenham Races at nearby
Prestbury, and as the western
gateway to the Cotswolds.

Proud it certainly is. Cheltenham
succeeded where others in the area
failed. From its humble beginnings
as a moderate little market town in
constant competition with
neighbouring Prestbury – each
inhibiting the growth of the other –
Cheltenham was virtually just a
single street in 1779, even though it
did stretch for almost a mile. Within
20 years its population had
quadrupled; within the 150 years it
had attracted some 60,000 more
inhabitants.

To the three p's should be added
a fourth – for pigeons – for the
success story of Cheltenham began

*Smart shops line one side of the
Promenade in Cheltenham.*

with pigeons. In what was, in 1716,
a meadow outside the little town
(and is now the Ladies' College) a
number of pigeons were found to be
pecking at what turned out to be salt
crystals at a spring. The owner
railed in the spot, raised a thatched
shed over it and gave Cheltenham
its first pump-room. Henry
Skillicorne, his astute son-in-law,
built a more permanent and
presentable edifice to house the
spring in 1748, improved the
approach to it and called it a spa.

Physicians wrote long treatises on
the medicinal virtues of the waters,
and George III stamped them with
the royal seal of approval by 'taking
them' in a five-week holiday at
Cheltenham in 1788. The shortage
of the waters soon afterwards
seemed like the demise which the
old radical, William Cobbett, had
hoped for. He saw the town as a sink
for plunderers and drunkards and
debauchees of all descriptions.
Others saw it as 'the favourite resort
of fashion and the shrine of health'.
New wells were sunk, the spa water
flowed and visitors arrived by the
trainload. The town put the pigeons
in its coat of arms.

AA recommends:
Hotels: Greenway, Shurdington,
1-rosette, 3 red star, *tel.* 862352
Prestbury House, The Burgage, Prestbury
(2m NE A46), 2-star, *tel.* 529533
Guesthouses: For a large selection of
guesthouses see the *AA Guesthouses,
Farmhouses & Inns in Britain* guide.
Garages: Bristol Street Motors,
83-93 Winchcombe Street, *tel.* 27061
Lex Mead, Princess Elizabeth Way,
tel. 20441 (day), 20440 (night)
Lyefield, 21-23 Lyefield Road West,
Charlton Kings, *tel.* 21131
Naunton Park (New Victory Mechanics),
Churchill Road, *tel.* 26979 (day), 20270
(night)

Chipping Campden

Map Ref: 83SP1539

On Campden wold the skylark sings,
In Campden town the traveller finds
The inward peace that beauty brings
To bless and heal tormented minds.

John Masefield certainly captured the essence of Chipping Campden, in the north Cotswolds, the most beautiful of all the market towns, for it wears its age with serenity and compels the visitor to slow down and take stock of its charm.

History in stone is the town's motto. Stone of honey-gold deepening to tawny-brown built the houses, shops, inns, tea-rooms and hotels standing shoulder to shoulder lining both sides of the long High Street. Steeply-pitched roofs, bold chimneys, gables and mullions, dormers and sundials and deep-set doorways pointed with shadow give them individual character.

The Church of St James stands at the westerly edge of the town; with its impressive pinnacled tower it is one of the most splendid of the Cotswold wool churches and is a veritable treasure-house of the town's past. The largest memorial brass in Gloucestershire is here – to William Grevel 'the flower of the wool merchants of all England'.

Church Street is a pocket of history. Close to the church are the Jacobean lodges and gateway – all that remains of the old manor of Campden. On the raised pavement is a row of almshouses built in the reign of King James I in stunning symmetry. The walled dip opposite is an old cartwheel wash.

On entering the High Street, Grevel House is on the right. Built in the 14th century it is distinguished by a Perpendicular bay window. Woolstaplers Hall on the left is a near contemporary and is now the town museum and tourist information centre.

The gabled Market Hall was built by Sir Baptist Hicks in 1627 to provide shelter for the stalls selling butter, cheese and poultry. The memorial cross and ancient town hall share its island in the middle of the High Street.

In Sheep Street is the old silk mill where C R Ashbee centred his Guild of Handicrafts – the Hart family of silversmiths continue the tradition today.

Tradition is strong in Chipping Campden. Its outstanding architecture is preserved by the Campden Trust, formed in 1929, which also fosters the craft movement. A separate society re-established the ancient Dover Games which take place on the hill above the town each Spring Bank Holiday.

The Jacobean Market Hall in the centre of the High Street at Chipping Campden was built by Sir Baptist Hicks, a wealthy benefactor of the town. Once used to shelter the butter and cheese stalls, it is now owned by the National Trust.

St James's Church, Chipping Campden. The oriental-looking lodges and gateway are all that remain of Hicks's house.

AA recommends:
Hotel: Kings Arms, The Square, I-rosette, I-star, tel. Evesham 840256

Chipping Norton

Map Ref: 85SP3127

Norton gained its Chipping, the medieval term for market, in the time of King John and evolved as a typical wool town with the traditional Perpendicular-style church as witness to its piety and prosperity. The rough justice of Henry VIII's day put the church to impious use when the town's vicar was hanged from the steeple for refusing to use Cranmer's English prayer book. St Mary's with its unusual hexagonal porch, has many fine features, but those in search of memorable monuments seek out the gravestone in the churchyard to Phillis, the wife of the rat-catcher.

Chipping Norton's most notable landmark is the tall chimney stack of Bliss Tweed Mill, an impressive Victorian building of an earlier mill producing tweeds outstanding for their durability. Bliss tweed cloth outlived its industry and the town's famous brewery and horse-blanket factory.

There is much in this little town that endures its changing economy: a row of gabled almshouses in Cotswold stone, Market Street and Middle Row where old buildings adapt to modern-day trading, and a splendid little theatre in Spring Street. A Town Trail, obtainable from the Tourist Centre, guides the visitor to the historic buildings and points of interest.

AA recommends:
Garage: Souch Autos, The Green, tel. 2656

DISCOVERY OF A ROMAN TESSELATED PAVEMENT, IN CIRENCESTER.

Cirencester

Map Ref: 93SP0201

The Romans called it Corinium; gentlefolk and country folk alike stick to Shakespeare's 'Cicester'; the indifferent say 'Siren'.

Only London was larger than Roman Corinium, which grew up at the intersection of the three major roads – the Foss Way, Ermin Way and Akeman Street.

Its strategic position on such a vital road junction and its sophistication did not impress the Saxons, who preferred to build smaller settlements outside the town walls, except for their church which was the longest parish church in England.

Cirencester regained its status under Norman rule for they realised the potential of its central position on the major trading routes, and it became the most important town in the Cotswolds for the medieval wool trade.

The pivot of modern Cirencester is the parish church – the largest in Gloucestershire and a splendid monument to the stonemasons' skills in an age when wealth and good taste went together. For all its splendour, it is the magnificent south porch which is the outstanding feature. Built by the abbots at the end of the 15th century as an office, it became the Town Hall after the Dissolution.

Cirencester parish church can also boast the oldest peal of 12 bells in England. And the tower observes some of the more ancient of campanological customs, including the ringing of the 'Pancake Bell' on Shrove Tuesday and the celebration of the Restoration at dawn on 29 May. From the top of the 162ft tower – the highest in Gloucestershire – the plan of the town can best be appreciated.

As with other towns, building and rebuilding has altered the overall complexion, but at ground level there is much charm to this country town. Stall-holders with their clutter and clamour fill the centre market-place; nice ladies produce nice preserves for the WI market; ancient hostelries range from horse brass-decked bars to Continental-style courtyards. Becoming rarer, and therefore more precious to the character of Cirencester, are the old established family butchers and bakers, coffee shops and ironmongers, florists and fishmongers and high-class jewellers, although a younger generation of craftsmen keeps old skills alive in a converted brewery.

Ancient buildings are preserved in such splendid examples as the Weavers Hall, the arches of St John's Hospital, Spitalgate, St Laurence's Almshouses and Coxwell Street. The only monastic survival is the Norman gatehouse in Grove Lane. 'Town Walks' by Civic Society guides are a great tourist feature.

The Abbey grounds are a delight, with swans on the Churn, the monks' gnarled old mulberry tree propped up alongside the path and acres of grass for the public to enjoy.

Cirencester Park, the seat of Lord Bathurst, is also open to the public, but the mansion, behind one of the largest yew hedges in the world, is not. The park is the finest surviving example in England of geometrical landscaping where great rides meet and grand vistas disappear into decreasing distances. Alexander Pope, who advised on its development, is remembered by a small rusticated stone shelter, called Pope's Seat. Polo, the game of royal princes, is regularly played at Cirencester Park.

AA recommends:
Hotels: King's Head, Market Place, 4-star, *tel.* 3322
Fleece, Market Place, 3-star, *tel.* 68507
Stratton House, Gloucester Road (A417), 3-star, *tel.* 61761
Self-catering: Trewsbury Holiday Cottages, *tel.* Kemble 306
Guesthouses: Raydon House Hotel, 3 The Avenue, *tel.* 3485
Rivercourt, Beeches Road, *tel.* 3998
La Ronde, 52-4 Ashcroft Road, *tel.* 4611
Wimborne, 91 Victoria Road, *tel.* 3890
Garage: Cirencester, Midland Road, Love Lane, *tel.* 3316 (day), 85591 (night)

A high semicircular yew hedge separates Cirencester House from the town

Cleeve Hill

Map Ref: 81SO9826

The A46 looping south-westwards from Winchcombe to Cheltenham follows the contour of Cleeve Hill as it juts its massive bulk out of the westerly escarpment.

Following the undulating course due south along the escarpment gives excellent views over the Vale of Gloucester with the famous Prestbury racecourse on the northern periphery of Cheltenham below. The summit at 1083ft is at the head of West Down at the southern point of the Common.

Cleeve Common on the high plateau is the gallops on which such famous jockeys as Fred Archer and Black Tom Oliver trained.

Along with Happy Valley, further south, Cleeve Common covers an area of some 3 square miles. It is a Site of Special Scientific Interest, scheduled as Grade I on account of its natural beauty.

Butterflies can be sent up in clouds on a good day; musk, frog and bee orchids are among the rarer of the wild flowers with the delicate harebell and hardy gorse providing strong contrasts. Sheep and cattle graze freely between the rough paths and bridle-tracks.

Cleeve Hill, looking to the Malverns.

Sheltering in an almost hidden valley below the north-easterly edge of the Common is the enchanting grouping of Jacobean manor-house, Tudor tithe barn and what is thought to be the oldest Roman Catholic chapel in the county. Postlip Hall, set in acres of unspoilt grounds, is sometimes open to the public. Higher up the valley and closer to the main road is Postlip Mill, the only surviving paper-making mill in the county.

AA recommends:
Hotel: Rising Sun, 2-star,
tel. Bishop's Cleeve 2002

The Cotswolds and their Golden Fleece

'In Europe the best wool is English; in England the best wool is Cotswold.' So ran the saying in Norman England, but the Cotswolds were exporting *fells* (the whole sheepskin on the hide of slaughtered animals) as early as AD 700 to English missionaries abroad.

Under Norman rule the export of wool increased considerably to meet the demands of the prestigious cloth industry of the Flemish weavers. Norman knights were rewarded for their services in the Conquest with vast estates, and they and the large numbers of monastic foundations increased their revenue by increasing their sheep-holdings. In the 20 years

The 'Cotswold Lions' are now kept at the Cotswold Farm Park near Guiting Power.

following the great Domesday census the sheep population outnumbered the people by four to one.

The Cotswold, the ancient breed descended from the Roman longwool sheep, thrived on the limestone-rich herbage to become the largest sheep in England. Named after the Cotswold hills (*cot* being a biblical term for enclosing sheep, and *wold* meaning rolling hillside) they grew long and heavy fleeces with strong curl and rich lustre. By the Middle Ages the whole Cotswold countryside was one vast sheepwalk.

Wealthy wool merchants rebuilt the old churches in Perpendicular style and enriched them with fine carvings and glorious stained glass windows. The finest examples of these wool churches are at Chipping Campden, Northleach, Cirencester, Fairford and Lechlade, where memorial brasses give some indication of the likeness of the old woolmen and their wives.

Wool became the most powerful political weapon. The wool merchants became creditors to the aristocracy and kings drew large incomes from the wool tax. The Chancellor was so delighted with the wool whose revenue accounted for over half of England's total wealth that he plumped himself down on a sack of Cotswold wool in Parliament. The Chancellor's seat is still a woolsack.

Eventually the taxes which raised the revenue crippled the wool trade. Cloth-making took over from sheep-farming and centred in the Stroud valleys where the abundant springs and strong water supply powered the mills. It was then the turn of the rich clothiers, who built fine houses for themselves in Cotswold style and of local stone, further enriching the architectural scene with domestic buildings.

The Industrial Revolution started the collapse, the introduction of synthetic fibres and the increased importation of cheaper cloths accelerated the decline of the once famous Cotswold woollen industry.

However, all is not history. Quality cloth is still produced in a couple of mills in the Stroud valley and across the Cotswolds in a converted stone barn at Filkins. The Cotswold Woollen Weavers card and spin and weave from the fleece, and visitors can see the processes for themselves amid the clack of shuttles, the rumble of looms and the evocative smells of machine oil and raw wool. And in small flocks on the rolling hill country can still be seen the Cotswolds, now a protected rare breed kept by keen members of the Cotswold Sheep Society.

THE COTSWOLD BREED

Coaley Peak and Frocester Hill Picnic Site

Map Ref: 78SO7901

Some 3 miles south-west of Stroud, on the B4066, Coaley Peak picnic site makes a fine point from which to explore the surrounding countryside as it is open all the year. Jointly owned and managed by the County Council and the National Trust, there is an information centre with display boards, illustrating the locality and its wildlife. Books are available on walks in the area.

Coaley Peak is typical of the limestone grassland to be found on the Cotswold scarp edge grazed in the summer months by a small flock of the ancient breed of Cotswold sheep. Within a short walking distance on Frocester Hill is Nympsfield Long Barrow.

The many Lords Berkeley successively enclosed lands around here by negotiation or force, any action brought by the commoners being 'to theire small comfort and less gaines'.

Coaley lies about a mile off; Frocester down its steep hill is a delightful vale village with a pretty gatehouse to its old Court. Frocester tithe barn is enormous, remarkable in both its construction and preservation for it dates back to around 1300.

An AA topograph on Frocester Hill identifies points of interest in the extensive views over the Severn Vale, Forest of Dean and the hills of Wales in the distance. A kissing-gate separates Coaley Peak from Frocester Hill.

AA recommends:
Guesthouse: Welches, Standish, *tel.* Stonehouse 2018

The AA topograph on Frocester Hill locates features of interest for the visitor. The view here is to Cam Long Down.

Cold Ashton

Map Ref: 78ST7472

The most southerly of the Cotswold hill villages, Cold Ashton, exposed to the prevailing sou'westerlies which blow straight off the Bristol Channel, is aptly named; but high up on the plateau above Bath the early medieval farmers established a vineyard on the south-facing slopes, and farms have grown round it ever since.

The church is perhaps more remarkable for having been largely rebuilt in Tudor times at the personal expense of the rector, rather than for any notable architectural merit. The Revd Thomas Key 'signed' his work both at the doorway and on a chantry window with the letter T entwined in a key. The oak pulpit has an exquisite stone canopy, quite rare in a Cotswold church and uncommonly beautiful.

It is the manor-house which attracts all the attention: Cold Ashton Manor has been described as the most perfect example of an Elizabethan house in all England. It is, unfortunately, not open to the public. From here, down the lovely St Catherine's Valley, the Limestone Link, a newly-opened footpath route, extends the Cotswold Way by 40 miles, winding through the hills beyond Bath to join the West Mendip Way.

AA recommends:
Hotel: Rudloe Park, Leafy Lane, Corsham, 3-star, *tel.* Hawthorn 810555
Self Catering: Cottage in the Garden, Colerne, *tel.* Box 742329

Cold Aston

Map Ref: 90SP1219

Cold Aston is often confused linguistically with Cold Ashton in the south Cotswolds, but apart from their exposed upland position (both stand at 700 feet above sea level) they have nothing else in common. Cold Aston has laboured under two names for over 400 years – and still does as can be seen on the signposts to and in the village.

Domesday is specific: *Eston* (Aston). Episcopal records are the first to qualify it as *frigida* in 1287, and it remained as such, or sometimes *cold* until 1554 when a Patent Roll announced the appointment of a vicar to *Aston Blank*. The right of presentation by then had passed to the Crown so for what reason the name was foisted on the village remains a mystery.

Aston Blank it became to church, education and postal authorities and the Inland Revenue. The inhabitants stoically stuck to Cold Aston, as did those who embroidered the church banners. The Ordnance Survey alternated the names on successive maps; the Highways Division plays safe and uses the alias.

Of paramount importance is the fact that it is a complete village; it has a shop and a school – rare

Georgian house on the green at Cold Aston.

facilities in small places today. On the tiny green stands a huge sycamore tree – one of the largest and oldest in England. The Norman church has no east window; a rare unaltered feature of early Celtic origin to be found in only four other Cotswold churches – Notgrove, Baunton, Winston and Brimpsfield. And, in the attractive 17th-century Plough Inn the question will still be asked: is this Cold Aston or Aston Blank?

Nature trail through the woods on Cooper's Hill. The trails are colour-coded; this one is yellow. The cheese-rolling contest takes place here in May.

The Colns

Map Ref: 94SP0810 and 95SP1405

The Coln, winding its way from the small Clevely brook off the high easterly slopes of Cleeve Hill to meet the Thames at Lechlade, runs through the heart of the Cotswolds. Three valley villages take their names from the river.

Coln St Dennis, the most northerly, is reached off the old Roman Foss Way, now the A429, at Fossebridge. A pocket-sized place of breath-taking simplicity, it is a honey-coloured Cotswold stone cluster of manor and farm, cottages and church. It takes its name from the church of St Dionisius of Paris to whom its lands were granted by William the Conqueror. The Norman church, with its modest squat tower, is dedicated to St James and stands in a tranquil spot on the riverside.

Coln Rogers, downstream, has work of even older hands to show, for its church retains a Saxon nave and chancel and quoining of its large stones in the long-and-short style. Originally known as Coln St Andrews, from the church dedication, the small village assumed the name Rogers from its patron, Roger de Gloucester, when he presented its living to that Abbey around 1100. West of the church an arched doorway to a shed-like ruin is possibly the remains of a 14th-century priest's house.

Coln St Aldwyns, separated from its upstream sisters by some six miles and the lovely village of Bibury, has the same charm but on a larger scale. This time it was the patron saint of the church which was changed. Formerly dedicated to the hermit saint, Ealdwine, the church favoured St John the Baptist in the 13th century.

The village radiates in four directions. Sturdy stone cottages set back in pretty gardens line the main street running north to south, with the gardens hiding to the rear as the cottages descend the hill to the old mill at the bottom. A magnificent chestnut tree stands sentinel as the east–west road crosses over at the top of the hill.

A cul-de-sac of manorial farm, barns and cottages groups with the church to the west; to the east is Williamstrip Park, the classical 17th-century mansion built in a commanding position over rolling parkland.

AA recommends:

Self Catering: Swyre Farm, Aldsworth, *tel.* Shipton-under-Wychwood 830252

Norman church at Coln St Dennis.

Cooper's Hill Local Nature Reserve

Map Ref: 86SO8914

Cooper's Hill owned by the County Council, is a massive spur of the west scarp edge about five miles south-east of Gloucester. The nature reserve of about 137 acres is within a larger area scheduled by the Nature Conservancy as a Site of Special Scientific Interest.

Its strategic position giving extensive views over the vale was realised as early as 500 BC when local tribes made it what was then one of the largest Iron Age encampments in the county.

Roman soldiers passed this way and, according to local tradition, left their ghosts behind them. A spring on the east side of the hill and a villa at nearby Witcombe are more settled and tangible evidence of their occupation.

A superb nature trail, passing through lovely woodland of beech, birch, sycamore and ash, and over open grassland to take in the vale views, is easily approached from Fiddler's Elbow on the A46, where there is space for parking.

The apex of the trail is the maypole on the northern tip, marking the point from where the Whitsuntide cheese-rolling race starts. The festival was once a hilarious mix of rustic revelry.

The programme of 1836 included dancing for the ribbons worn by the Master of Ceremonies, *shimey to be ron for* (girls raced for the prize of a chemise), and *a bladder of snuff to be chatred for by hold wimming* (the old woman who chattered the longest and loudest won the snuff). The races down (and one up) the hill are still included today in a much more decorous, but still colourful, custom. From the maypole on a clear day can be seen May Hill to the left, backed by the smudgy outline of the Black Mountains; the misty mauve of the Malverns some 20 miles ahead and the bluff of Cleeve Cloud above Cheltenham to the right.

Ralph Vaughan Williams

From the 'English Hymnal' By permission of the Oxford University Press.

Down Ampney.   6.6.11. D.   R. VAUGHAN WILLIAMS.

Down Ampney appears above the hymn 'Come down, O Love Divine' in the Church of England's English Hymnal 1906. It is the title of the music composed by Dr Ralph Vaughan Williams and commemorates his birthplace in the south-eastern corner of the Cotswolds.

Born on 12th October 1872 at the Old Vicarage — which was then only seven years old — Ralph Vaughan Williams was the youngest of three children of the vicar, Arthur Charles Vaughan Williams and his wife Margaret, daughter of Josiah Wedgwood III.

He was only three years old when his father died and his mother returned to the family home in Surrey where the children were brought up. A stained glass window was inserted in the old stone Church of All Saints in memory of the young vicar, who is buried close to the south porch in the quiet churchyard touching the wood-edged fields at one end of the village of Down Ampney.

Initially educated at home, Vaughan Williams went to preparatory school, where he showed an early aptitude for the violin and pianoforte. At Charterhouse he progressed to the viola and organ and entered the Royal College of Music in 1890. Later, while at Trinity College, Cambridge, he continued his weekly lessons with Sir Hubert Parry. In 1908 he studied with Ravel in Paris.

During the years 1902–12 Dr Vaughan Williams collected traditional folk-songs, writing the words and notes of the tune as the singer sang in the harvest field, or in a cottage or the local inn — a laborious task which he obviously undertook in the light of what he said had been inculcated in him by his old teacher, Max Bruch,

'you must not write eye music; you must write ear music'.

His symphonies and folk-songs alike were in characteristically English style, earning him the respect and admiration of music-lovers everywhere and the Order of Merit from George V.

Although fate and fame kept him in London, Vaughan Williams was frequently in the Cotswolds; he followed William Morris at Broadway, and the ancient drove roads, such as the Welsh Way, feature in his Cotswold opera *Hugh the Drover*. He composed for and conducted several times at the Three Choirs Festival at Gloucester, and just two years before his death attended a production at the Cheltenham College. Gustav Holst, his closest friend from their student days, was born at Cheltenham.

When Vaughan Williams died in 1958, he was buried in Westminster Abbey, and the music that accompanied the procession to the grave was the one which he had composed to honour his Cotswold birthplace — Down Ampney.

Cranham

Map Ref: 86SO8912

The village settles in a deep hollow of ancient beech woods, named by the Saxons. Where they reach out to the high escarpment near Birdlip they hide the source from which the River Frome springs.

The Church of St James overlooks the village. Two pairs of sheep-shears are carved on the tower, symbols of the wool trade whose merchants built the church. Hands of all centuries have furnished it but it was the Victorians who enlarged it.

Cranham is one of the beauty spots of the Cotswolds and its annual Feast and Ox Roast is a typical village affair attracting visitors from far and wide each August.

Crickley Hill Country Park

Map Ref: 86SO9316

Crickley Hill is a promontory of the escarpment. It overshadows the A417 as it leaves the Air Balloon public house on the corner to descend to Gloucester.

The hill-fort to the south-west of the park is the site of one of the most important archaeological discoveries in Europe. Reconstructions and artefacts, guided tours and lectures demonstrate the history of the hill's inhabitants from the Stone Age farmers who lived there for 1,000 years, first in their long houses, later in round houses, and so to the Roman

Rosebay willowherb growing at Crickley Hill Country Park.

occupation. Each summer the hill is alive with the babble of a dozen languages as volunteers (3,000 have taken part since 1969) continue the long task of excavation under the educational charity trust.

Daglingworth and the Duntisbournes

Map Ref: 93SO9708 to 93SO9905

The Saxons came off the Roman Ermin Way (A417) to this sequestered valley three miles north-east of Cirencester, and, at Daglingworth, much of their stonemasons' skill remains – in a sundial over the church doorway and a Crucifixion scene on the exterior of the chancel. Holy Rood Church stands on a bank above the village, which clusters in groups,

like gossips, on both sides of the stream. The manor forms its own nucleus at Lower End, with a circular medieval dovecote among the traditional angles of houses large and small.

The Duntisbournes nestle in knots upstream. Tucked into the fold of the wooded hill valley, they take their name from the Duntisbourne brook which knits them together with Daglingworth before it joins the Churn.

Duntisbourne Rouse is an idyllic spot caught in a hollow of green hills, with a ford in the bottom and a saddleback-towered church on a steep bank.

Middle Duntisbourne, settled around another ford, is a farming hamlet of Duntisbourne Leer, itself a hamlet of Duntisbourne Abbots.

Fleurs-de-lys carved on chimney and doorhead of a farmhouse and the Leer in its name echo the manor's early ownership by the Abbey of Lire in Normandy.

Duntisbourne Abbots, possessed by St Peter's Abbey of Gloucester, perpetuates those early ties in the names of the village and dedication of its church. Unusual centre-pivoted gates make true use of the lych-gate. A youth hostel is a modern amenity in this old valley village.

Down Ampney

Map Ref: 94SU1097

Separated from the other three Ampney villages by some 4 miles of flat meadowlands, Down Ampney has an almost suburban appearance with its house-lined long street. Newly-built houses infill the gaps between old cottages, and gardens grow smaller in consequence.

At the very end of the village, in a peaceful tree-shaded corner, is the medieval Down Ampney House, its Tudor gatehouse seen now only in

The Vicarage at Down Ampney. It was here that Ralph Vaughan Williams spent the first three years of his life.

old engravings. All Saints Church is a venerable neighbour, furnished with the work of many centuries.

Down Ampney is a place of pilgrimage to honour its past heroes. Sir Nicholas Villiers is shown in coat-of-mail, as befits a Crusader. Today's Knights Hospitallers return each year adding a touch of pageantry to this quiet spot.

World War II airmen are commemorated in a stained-glass window in the church, a plaque at the end of the runway from which they flew and an annual service; and music lovers pause reverently at the gate of the Old Vicarage – the birthplace of Vaughan Williams.

Dursley

Map Ref: 78ST7597

Dursley's early manorial ties with the powerful Berkeleys, who held the long-lost castle there, were severed as the town turned from its feudal masters to seek new prosperity in the woollen industry.

Depressed but by no means defeated by the decline in woollen manufacture, the mill owners put their industrial expertise into new enterprises. Engineering development from metalsmiths and Listers of Dursley, who first came to the town to serve the weaving mills, must be the success story of the century, producing everything from diesel engines to sheep-shears.

The 15th-century Church of St James, built of local tufa, had its tower rebuilt in 1707–1709 after the collapse of the original tower and spire.

Streets with the history of the town wrapped up in their names

branch out from the central Market Place. The Market House has a bell in its turret and Queen Anne in a niche holding centre-stage. A literary circle to the east of the town at Whiteway comprises roads dedicated to Wordsworth, Byron, Kipling, Tennyson and Chaucer, with Shakespeare Road the longest, presumably on account of his short stay in the town in 1585 when he was sought by the Lord of the Manor not for his talents as a poet but as a poacher!

Roads leading westward out of the town rise steeply along the Broadway to Stinchcombe Hill, an

Golfers on Stinchcombe Hill, just outside Dursley.

18-hole golf course and an area open to the public.

The views from the top are superb. You can see Exmoor on a clear day, the misty mauve of the Malverns and the brooding Brecon Beacons in the far distance. Closer to the Cotswolds scene are the rugged and ragged edges of the western scarpline to the north and south, with tantalising glimpses of the secret wooded ways of Waterley Bottom and Owlpen and Stinchcombe village below.

AA recommends:

Guesthouses: Drakestone House, Stinchcombe (farmhouse) (2½m W off B4060), *tel.* 2140
Park, Stancombe Park, Dursley (farmhouse), *tel.* 45345

Dyrham Park was extensively rebuilt by William Blaythwayt, Secretary of State to William III, after the death of his wife, who had inherited the estate.

Dyrham Park

Map Ref: 78ST7375

Deer, which gave Dyrham its name, are still to be seen in the deer park sloping down to the great manor-house built by William Blathwayt, Secretary of State to William III.

The towering hillside, enclosed by the steep escarpment of the southern Cotswolds, affords panoramic views over the south-west extending as far as Bristol. The same hills once landscaped in terraces with gardens below, were without parallel in England. The 264 acres of Dyrham House, are now owned by the National Trust.

The manor-house exemplifies the fabric and furnishings of the late 17th century; a housekeeper's inventories fill in the gaps. The house is closed during the winter, but the Deer Park is open all year.

Next door to the manor-house is the parish church of the peaceful little village of Dyrham. Dyrham holds a special place in history for one of the most decisive battles on English soil was fought here in 577 when the Saxons gained control of Gloucester, Cirencester and Bath. The site of the battle on Hinton Hill is made more prominent by a plantation of conifers.

Toghill, to the south, overtopping Freezing Hill opposite, is on the Cotswold scarp line. The picnic area, with car park, corners into the point where the A420 meets the ancient Jurassic Way – named after the limestone rock ridgeway stretching from Bath to the Humber.

Fairford

Map Ref: 95SP1500

'Faireforde never flourished afore ye Tames came to it', wrote Leland, antiquary to Henry VIII, of this Coln valley market town in the south-east corner of the Cotswolds.

It is to old John Tame's church, St Mary's, focal point of the main street, that visitors have been attracted for five centuries. The magnet is the only complete set of medieval stained glass windows to survive in the whole of the British Isles. Their design is now generally attributed to Barnard Flower, 'Master Glass Painter' to Henry VII. This is borne out by the fact that John Tame, a wealthy wool merchant, who rebuilt the church and endowed it with the magnificent windows, was a tenant of the Tudors and everywhere in the fine 'wool' church is to be seen the Tudor rose carving. It is to the windows that the eye is constantly drawn – locally and anciently they were known as 'the poor man's bible', depicting in glowing jewel-like colours the pictoral story of the entire Catholic faith.

South of the noble church is the former school, an endowment of three ladies of the manor, of which Elizabeth Farmor was the greatest benefactor and from whom the school took its name. Farmor's moved to new buildings in the park, on the site of the old manor-house, in 1961, and the substantial stone building is now the community centre. Contiguous to the old school is Fairford House, an elegant contemporary building on the site of the Tames' family house.

The Bull Hotel, flanks the entire west side of the market-place, ending in a half-timbered building, formerly the George Inn. The White Hart, opposite, with even older foundations, narrows the corner where the main road runs through the town.

The mainly 18th-century High Street reflects the prosperity of the age when Fairford was a major posting town on the Gloucester to London coach run. Sandwiched between Park Street with its medieval dovecote and cottages all in a row prettily aproned with tiny gardens and London Street on the A417 is the Croft with the county's smallest cottage hospital. The famous Fairford Carnival which had once financed its running has now been replaced by an annual Steam Rally in mid-August.

The Coln separates the ancient borough from the old 'milltown' west end – a rural expanse of meadow and mill – terminated by a mix of farm and residential area on the site of an ancient Saxon settlement.

Filkins

Map Ref: 79SP2404

Cotswold Woollen Weavers is the sign that catches the eye of motorists speeding along the A361 between Burford and Lechlade. The sinuous route along which the packhorses and wool-laden waggons trundled over the centuries from the markets of Campden to the docks at Southampton has now been bypassed and the little village of Filkins cut off from arterial traffic.

Filkins is just over the county border in Oxfordshire. Its character is totally Cotswold, built from locally quarried stone. Stone is the outstanding feature of Filkins. The huge rectangular slabs fastened

Weaving using traditional machinery by the Cotswold Woollen Weavers at Filkins.

together with iron clamps came from the Long Ground Quarry; peculiar to Filkins, they edge the cottage gardens looking for all the world like thin and hoary headstones. One *slat*, for the slabs are really Cotswold stone tiles, completely roofs the old village lock-up, twinned cosily to the tiny cottage which houses the most incredible local collection to be found anywhere. Formed through the acquisitive acumen of its oldest inhabitant, stonemason George Swinford, and the philanthropic foresight of its greatest benefactor, Sir John Cripps, Filkins Museum was the model for the University of Reading's great Museum of Country Life.

The whole village concept is a model of how initiative and enterprise can be engineered into making rural areas thriving communities again. Craft workshops have settled into disused farm buildings at the end of the village: rush weavers, a furniture restorer and a stonemason have already joined the woollen weavers, who spin, card and weave in a beautiful 18th-century Cotswold barn.

Gloucester

Map Ref: 86SO8417

It was while holding court at Gloucester that William I had 'deep speech with his Witan' – resulting in the great Domesday survey. For centuries this old city has stood guardian on the strategic point of the Severn, gateway to the West and the Cotswold hill country above it, and the Conqueror followed the custom of Edward the Confessor, who also held his court in Gloucester for Christmas.

It was the Saxons who divided the country into administrative shires,

and Gloucester has been the capital of its shire from those times. Of their age little remains, and so completely did the Romans drive the old Britons from this spot that only Roman Glevum is revealed to the excavators.

The Normans reshaped the Saxon monastery to become an abbey, which grew into the great cathedral built as a cross; its imposing tower rises 225 feet above the city – pinnacles and open tracery catching the light and the attention for miles around. The great east window of Gloucester Cathedral is virtually a wall of glowing glass and is the largest medieval window in the kingdom; the misericords are an artistic romp through the fables; and the stone embroidery of fan-tracery is exquisite.

Centred round the ancient Cross, the city radiates north, south, east and west, the streets taking their names from the gates of the walls which the Normans had built on Roman foundations.

The walled city played a prominent part in the turmoil of the Civil War and, despite a month of mining and tunnelling, the besieged garrison, down to its last three barrels of gunpowder, resisted the Royalist attack. Edward Massey, who held the city, changed sides and supported Charles II. At the Restoration he was elected MP for Gloucester and the new king ordered the city walls to be levelled.

Elizabeth I granted Gloucester the dignity of a port. The docks, which played such a vital role in the Midlands, are being revitalised as part of the plans to maintain a working balance of history and

The figures of Father Time, a Welshwoman, a Scotsman, John Bull and an Irishwoman chime the hours above a clock shop in Southgate Street, Gloucester.

The three-masted sailing ship, the Saracen, in Gloucester docks.

industry, commerce and the arts, business and recreational pursuits, in a modern city with a medieval heart.

AA recommends:
Guesthouses: Alma, 49 Kingsholm Road, tel. 20940
Claremont, 135 Stroud Road, tel. 29540
Lulworth, 12 Midland Road, tel. 21881
Monteith, 127 Stroud Road, tel. 25369
Rotherfield House Hotel, 5 Horton Road, tel. 410500
Garages: Page & Davies, 56a Barton Street, Eastgate, tel. 720332 (day), 32863 (night)
Painswick Road, Matson, tel. 29866 (day), 856608 (night)
Westgate Motorhouse Company, 209–211 Westgate Street, tel. 34581

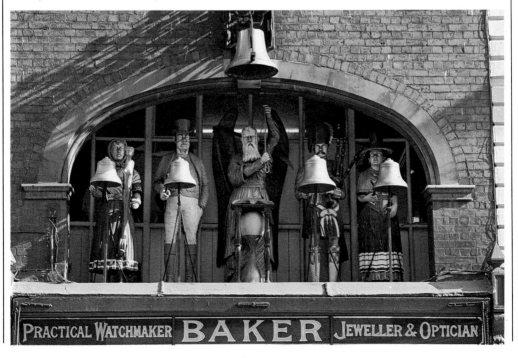

PRACTICAL WATCHMAKER **BAKER** JEWELLER & OPTICIAN

Guiting Power and Cotswold Farm Park

Map Ref: 89SP0924 and 83SP1126

The Guitings take their name from their position on the upper reaches of the Windrush in the north Cotswolds. *Gyte* is Old English for 'flood' and Power was the name of the local family. Guiting Power was originally called Nether Guiting from its siting lower down the valley from its twin, Temple Guiting – so distinguished by belonging to the Knights Templar.

Farms are dotted along the banks where the streams from Guiting Wood and the willow-lined valley meet, and sturdy cottages close in on the picturesque village green.

In the heart of quarry-land, Guiting Power has made good use of its stone in simple and traditional style, its attraction being that of grouping by purpose rather than for individual design.

Above the village, on the open rolling wolds is Bemborough Farm, the centre and shop window of the Rare Breeds Survival Trust.

Cotswold Farm Park is an adjunct to the working farm and since its opening in 1970 has drawn families and students, conservationists, television, film crews and the press to see the ancient breeds of farm animals and fowl in a natural farm environment. Here you can see the Cotswold sheep, which once carried the wealth of medieval England on their backs; the Old Gloucester cows, whose rich milk made the famous Double Gloucester cheese; and the Gloucester Old Spot pigs, which survived on old-fashioned farms where they were left to forage freely in the orchards, thereby producing distinctive, apple-flavoured hams!

Seaweed-eating Orkneys, oxen, cattle, boars, goats and every endangered species of British farm animal are of interest to the visitor and serve a serious purpose in the fight for survival. Educational facilities are an important feature of

Gloucester Old Spot sow and piglets. One of the rare breeds of farm animals at the Cotswold Farm Park.

the Farm Park with seasonal attractions such as sheep-shearing and special exhibitions. A children's corner is a great favourite, where tiny tots can roam freely with tiny animals.

Hailes

Map Ref: 82SP0430

Hailes is a hauntingly beautiful ruin of an abbey once so magnetic that it drew royalty and pilgrims alike to this remote little spot.

Winchcombe was already a powerful monastic seat by the time of the Conquest, and when Ralph de Worcester fortified a small castle at Hailes and built a church in about 1130 the Abbot of Winchcombe clawed in a compensatory pension of seven shillings a year and exercised a considerable measure of dominance over the church. This simple building, no larger than a barn, has medieval paintings on the walls, heraldic tiles on the floor, and a tranquillity that only 800 years endow.

Winchcombe was no doubt more incensed but powerless to intervene when Hailes was chosen as the site for a new monastery for the Cistercian Order.

As a thanksgiving for having survived a shipwreck, Richard, Earl of Cornwall and King of the Romans, built the magnificent abbey on land granted for the purpose by his brother Henry III. Consecrated in 1251, Hailes attracted rich and poor, the noble, the infirm and the penitent after Edmund, Earl Richard's son, presented the abbey with a phial authenticated as containing the

Fine 13th-century vaulting boss showing Christ as a spiritual Samson rending the lion's jaw, Hailes Abbey Museum.

Beatrix Potter in the Cotswolds

And the queerest thing about it is — I heard it in Gloucestershire, and it is true! at least the tailor, the waistcoat, and the "No more twist".'

The Tailor of Gloucester, which Beatrix Potter called 'my own favourite amongst the little books', was written as a Christmas present in 1901 for her little friend called Freda Moore.

It was while visiting her cousins, Judge Crompton Hutton and his family, at Harescombe Grange, near Stroud, that Beatrix Potter first heard the story 'from Miss Caroline Hutton, who had it of Miss Lucy of Gloucester, who had it of the tailor'.

The tailor who was the centre of the ladies' gossip at their tea-party was then a very young man, John Prichard of Gloucester, who had been commissioned to make a special waistcoat for the new mayor to wear in an important procession through the city.

The tailor was very busy and the great day was nearly upon him. On the Saturday he left his tailor's shop with the special waistcoat only just cut out. When he returned on the Monday he was astonished to find it finished — except for one buttonhole. A little note pinned to it said, 'No more twist'. The tailor could not understand how the work had been done so he put the waistcoat in his window with a sign 'Come to Prichard where the waistcoats are made at night by the fairies!'.

Beatrix Potter was fascinated by the story for she delighted in fairy-tales. She changed the fairies to mice, the young busy tailor to an old and poor man, and the civic occasion of the Root, Fruit and Grain Society Show to the Mayor's Wedding.

In Gloucester she sat on doorsteps sketching streets and buildings, and the ancient archway of Cathedral Close. She visited homes in Stroud to sketch cottage interiors: a bed with hangings, a dresser filled with crockery and a hob fire grate. At Harescombe Grange she used the coachman's son as a model for her tailor. The Tate Gallery chose her original Tailor of Gloucester pictures for an exhibition, and the story has enthralled millions, of all ages, across the world.

The mystery of the waistcoat was later revealed by the tailor's two

The House of The Tailor of Gloucester (below) with Beatrix Potter books and memorabilia, and its sign (above right).

assistants who had let themselves into the workshop secretly to do their master's work. The tailor, John Prichard, later became a teacher and lived at Haresfield. He died in 1934 and his tombstone records that he was the tailor of Gloucester.

The House of The Tailor of Gloucester is a tiny shop at 9 College Court, built on to the stone wall of Cathedral Close, the fictional home of the tailor. It is a fascinating centre devoted to the Beatrix Potter range of books and gifts. A working model of the mice, a real old-fashioned hob-grate, dresser and tailor's chair are at the back of the shop in a recreated kitchen, faithful to her illustrations. The Gloucestershire Federation of the Women's Institute embroidered the exquisite waistcoat, modelled on the same waistcoat in the Victoria and Albert Museum which Beatrix Potter had used as her model.

The House of The Tailor of Gloucester is open every weekday 9.30 to 5.30 — admission free.

---

blood of Christ but later found to be false. The main buildings were destroyed in the Dissolution of the Monasteries in 1539.

Graceful arches and stony outlines of the ground plan are all that remain of the building, but in

Early 16th-century tile pavement in Hailes Abbey Museum.

the adjacent museum there are many exhibits excavated from the site to indicate its former glory.

Haresfield Beacon

Map Ref: 78SO8208

About three miles north-west of Stroud, Haresfield Beacon, a promontory at the tip of Ring Hill, is

perhaps the most notable of the summits along the Cotswold escarpment. A National Trust car park at the north end of Standish Wood allows easy access to the hill.

Haresfield Hill and Beacon are famous as viewpoints from which the Berkeley Vale can be seen as a pastoral panorama. In the middle distance are the silvery waters of the Severn making a spectacular loop around Arlingham before broadening out into a shining sheet as the tidal waters flow down to swell those of the Wye at Chepstow. The dark expanse of the Forest of Dean makes an impressive backdrop.

From the Severn the lush green pastures and fruitful fields of the vale are rolled out as a carpet, 700 feet below the beacon.

The geological outliers of Robins Wood Hill and Churchdown Hill can be easily spotted either side of the city of Gloucester. A closer look at the narrowing of the isthmus illustrates how Haresfield too has been detached from the limestone mass to become yet one more of the Cotswolds' outlying hills.

Within the wood-edged bulk of Haresfield Hill Romans made use of an ancient hill-fort and stowed away a hoard of some 3000 coins.

Hidcote

Map Ref: 83SP1742

A tiny tributary of the Knee brook to the west of Moreton Vale, almost severs Hidcote Hill from the Cotswolds, but it is not an outlier in the same sense as is Meon Hill, the outpost just to the north. Its character is that of the Gloucestershire Cotswolds built in golden limestone on the south Midland clay.

The twin hamlets of Hidcote Boyce and Bartrim are both pretty and evocative of the heart of England. Hidcote derives from Old English *cote* or *cot* meaning cottages and speaks of its smallness from early times; the hamlets are distinguished by the addition of the names of their respective feudal tenants.

It is to Hidcote Bartrim, 4 miles north-east of Chipping Campden and 1 mile east of the A46, that visitors are drawn, for, secluded

Hidcote Manor Gardens (main picture) and a view looking through to the pool garden (inset).

down the leafy country lanes, surrounded by its own farm and thatched cottages is Hidcote Manor and one of Britain's most delightful gardens.

A garden of gardens separated by hedges, Hidcote was created early this century by the great horticulturist, Major Lawrence Johnston, and is now in the care of the National Trust. Its 10 acres are carefully planned winter borders and spring slopes, camellia corners and rock banks, terraces and long walks, circles and dells, avenues of pine, lime, oak and holly, and walks where roses ramble, linking the six major gardens, each on a theme of colour, shape or scent.

A Shakespearean production is staged each summer on the Theatre Lawn, and from the top of the garden there are splendid views over the woods and meadows of the valley westward to Bredon Hill. Shakespeare's Stratford-upon-Avon is just 10 miles away.

Close by to the south-east is the thatched stone cottage village of Ebrington with a church dating back to Norman times. To the north-west lie the thatched timber-

framed cottages of Mickleton, the home of the Graves family, the most famous of which was Richard – declared to be one of the best writers of the late 18th century.

AA recommends:
Garage: D & M Fancutt, 35 High Street, Honeybourne, *tel.* Evesham 830382

Kelmscot

Map Ref: 79SU2499

'*. . . And Thames runs chill*
twixt mead and hill
But kind and dear
is the old house here . . .'

The old house for which William Morris wrote this poem is Kelmscot Manor, in his own words a 'many-gabled old house built by the simple countryfolks of the long-past times'.

His home for the last 25 years of his life, the majestic old Elizabethan manor (occasionally open to the public) is set in the south-eastern

corner of the Cotswolds on the banks of the Upper Thames. It is filled with his works and Rossetti's art. A delightful domestic touch is the valance on Morris's oak four-poster displaying his poem *For the bed at Kelmscott*, embroidered by his daughter, May.

Kelmscot village is, in part, a memorial to William Morris: a stone-carving on the Memorial Cottages, designed by Philip Webb, showing Morris sitting in the home mead under bird-filled trees is itself a work of art; the Morris Memorial Hall, designed by Ernest Gimson, was opened by George Bernard Shaw. Nearby is the old Plough Inn, a favourite meeting place for the river travellers who stop off at this quiet farming village.

AA recommends:
Guesthouses: Bampton House, Bushey Row, Bampton, *tel.* Bampton Castle 850135
Morar Weald Street, Bampton (½m SW off A4095) (farmhouse), *tel.* Bampton Castle 850162

Lechlade

Map Ref: 95SU2199

'Clear Coln and Lively Leche go down
   from Cotteswold's plain,
At Lechlade joining hands, come
   likewise to support
The mother of great Thames.'

Lechlade takes its name from the Leach and its fame from the Thames. It is the cornerstone of south-east Gloucestershire, meeting the old counties of Wiltshire, Oxfordshire and Berkshire on its boundary bridges.

St John's Bridge, the oldest, on the A417 Lechlade to Faringdon road, has stood since 1228 close to the confluence of the Leach and the Thames. The Augustinian hospital, founded on the site of what is now the Trout Inn, gave its name to the old bridge, the street leading to it and St John's Lock, marking the highest navigable reaches of the Thames.

The view upstream is a glorious juxtaposition of brightly-painted boats bobbing busily through the lock amid the pastoral peace of water-meadows, with the 'dim and distant spire' of St Lawrence's church in the background. Shelley composed his *Summer Evening Meditation* in 1815 in Lechlade churchyard, where Sarah, the first wife of Robert Raikes the founder of the Sunday School movement, is buried.

A monumental brass to a wool merchant, with his feet on a woolsack, pays tribute to the trade upon which the fine 'wool' church was built. Its re-dedication to a Spanish saint was in deference to Katherine of Aragon, who held the manor in the early 16th century.

The church makes a striking

Pleasure craft have superseded the working boats that once plied the Thames from Lechlade, carrying Cotswold stone to London.

corner-piece to the triangular market-place, which has the main road running across its base. The Old Vicarage rambles along one side, the library and police station, replacing older houses, on the other, ending with the old, maid-haunted, red-brick New Inn. The great arched carriageway is a reminder of the town's busy coaching past and affords a glimpse through it of the river.

Halfpenny Bridge, arching over the Thames on the A361 Lechlade to Swindon road, was built in the 18th century and has a tiny square tollhouse on the brow. The old wharf below now teems with pleasure craft. Sleek cruisers set off downstream to Buscot and beyond, while creaking rowing-boats weave their own somnolent course upstream to explore the water-weedlands up to the Round House, where the old canal once brought the Severn to the Thames.

Marshfield

Map Ref: 78ST7773

103 miles from Hyde Park Corner, as a plaque in the High Street confirms, is the town turned village of Marshfield. Its Cotswold identity is shown boldly in rows of gabled stone-roofed houses, fine old inns and a manorial group of church, farm, barn and dovecote. Marshfield marks the easterly point of Cotswold's southerly hill edge, the pinnacled tower of St Mary's making a distinguished landmark high up above the Avon vale.

Its position on the ridge, 600 feet above sea level, is a natural boundary point. An ancient-looking megalithic arrangement of three huge stones marks the meeting of the three counties of Gloucestershire, Wiltshire and Somerset.

Marshfield's market charter was obtained 700 years ago and, true to Cotswold tradition, traded on the wool and corn of its farmland. Its importance in the coaching era, as the first or last posting town on the Bristol to London run, and its proximity to Bath, is reflected in a dozen hostelries of 18th-century origin. The romance of the horse-drawn age is spiced by the tale of Dick Turpin making Star Farm one of his highway hold-up haunts.

Unlike many other wool towns, Marshfield did not decline with the trade but channelled its resources into malting. Some 80 malt houses were at one time supplying the breweries at Bath and Bristol. A number of fine Queen Anne-style houses with distinctive shell-hooded doorways were built by the prosperous maltsters and add an elegant touch to the extremely long High Street, which stretches east to west from the market-place to the old almshouses, with the removed and rebuilt Tolzey Hall inbetween as a reminder of the village's former borough status.

Since the A420 bypassed it in the Sixties and the M4 cut above it four miles away in the Seventies, major roads no longer go through it, but at Christmastide folks flock to the village to see the Marshfield Mummers. The seven characters, distinctively dressed in costumes covered in strips of newspaper and coloured papers, play out their ancient ritual based on the fight of St George and the Dragon.

AA recommends:
Self Catering: Cottage in the Garden, Colerne, *tel.* 742329

Minchinhampton

Map Ref: 92SO8700

Minchinhampton, a populous medieval parish which stretched between the valleys of Chalford and Nailsworth, became a busy little market town in the mid-13th century. Its development followed closely that of the Cotswold wool and cloth trades. Sheep were farmed on the high plateau pasture lands and the wool was turned to cloth in the mills of the valley bottoms.

Its early existence accounts for its traditional building style; all is stone-built and all is in unison. The market square has a fine Market House supported on stone columns, there are many fine houses of considerable age, and, something which few places can boast, a Queen Anne post office.

On the north side is Minchinhampton Common where a crowd of around 20,000 assembled on foot and horseback to hear George Whitefield preach on a tump in 1743, despite his having been assaulted in the town.

High up on the plateau, the Common, the second largest in the Cotswolds, is a spacious stretch of primeval England. Selsey Hill can be seen to the south, Haresfield Beacon to the west, and close-cropped turf for as far as the eye can

Giving the horses a long rein after a gallop on Minchinhampton Common.

see. Golfers and riders, picnickers and kite-flyers, loose ponies and cattle all make their own ways across the 580 acres, now in the hands of the National Trust.

The Tingle Stone, with the big hole in its centre through which rickety children were passed by superstitious mothers, stands close to the entrance to Gatcombe Park, the home of Princess Anne where horse trials are frequently staged.

Minster Lovell

Map Ref: 79SP3111

Minster Lovell, an enchanting stone and thatch village on a narrow lane off the Burford to Witney road, is a place to linger. The old church is set above the river and was built by William Lovell, whose effigy in armour is a fine example of 15th-century work in alabaster; but it is the ruins of the manor-house which he built that hold the centre-stage.

Stately in its ruin, Minster Lovell manor-house must have been splendid in its prime, as can be seen from plans and old engravings which reconstruct its former magnificence.

The ruined manor and church at Minster Lovell.

Francis, 13th Lord Lovell, sought refuge here after fighting for Lambert Simnel. His whereabouts was known only to a trusted servant who met with an accident, leaving his master to die trapped and starved. Repairs to the house in 1708 revealed the skeletons of a man and a dog in a secret chamber.

Tragedy struck again when a young Lovell bride climbed into an old oak chest in one of the manor's many rooms during a game of hide-and-seek as part of the Christmas wedding festivities. The heavy lid closed on her firm and fast, and the coffer became her coffin. The tragic tale has survived the centuries in the ballad 'The Mistletoe Bough'.

A quite different chapter of social history was written on the south side of the main road. Marked Charterville Allotments on the map, the settlement was one of the five Chartist estates founded by the famous radical, Feargus O'Connor, whose lottery plan for house and land ownership startled the Victorians and excites today's historians.

AA recommends:
Hotel: Old Swan, 2-star, *tel.* Witney 75614
Guesthouse: Hill Grove (farmhouse), *tel.* Witney 3120

Moreton-in-Marsh

Map Ref: 84SP2032

Only three counties now meet at the old Four Shire stone near Moreton-in-Marsh, a sizeable grey stone market town on the Foss Way in the north Cotswolds.

Originally part of Blockley parish, Moreton derives from 'farmstead on the moor' and gained its affix in the 13th century as *Henmarsh*. An infuriating erroneous interpretation is 'in-the-Marsh'. The *Marsh* is more properly a corruption of *March*, meaning boundary.

The oldest part of the town is settled round the church, originally a chapel of ease for nearby Bourton-on-the-Hill. There was much rebuilding of both St David's Church, with a fine tower of golden ashlar, and the older buildings in Victorian times.

Transport determined the growth of Moreton-in-Marsh more than any other factor. The improvement of the road system, following the course of the Romans' rigidly direct route, brought the coaching trade through and to the town. The Redesdale Arms, formerly called the Unicorn, the Manor House and the White Hart – with the tradition that Charles I slept there in 1644 – date back to the principal inns of that era.

However, it was the age of steam that brought Moreton its greatest prosperity. The town increased in size by half as much again when the railway opened up new arteries of trade. One of the few horse railways on the Cotswolds opened in 1826 to run from Moreton 16 miles northward to Stratford on its navigable River Avon. Ten years later a branch line opened to Shipston-on-Stour, and 15,000 tons of coal were hauled along these tracks in each of its boom years. Steam replaced horse power in 1889 and by 1904 the line had fallen out of use. An increase in building continues and the town has expanded this century to the east and south.

The centre of the High Street is the Market Hall, sharing its island with the Mann Institute, inscribed with Ruskin's lovely line, 'Every noble life leaves the fibre of it interwoven for ever in the work of the World'. It is fitting that this should be at Moreton, for here is the great fire-fighting training centre.

A curious coincidence to this most modern and advanced service

The broad main street of Moreton-in-Marsh lies on the route of the Roman Foss Way.

is that Moreton is one of the few places to boast a curfew tower. It has stood on the corner of Oxford Street for four centuries. Curfew dates back to the Norman Conquest when a bell was rung to warn townsfolk to 'cover-fire' for the night. The curfew bell, dated 1633, was rung at Moreton-in-Marsh until 1860.

About 1½ miles to the north-west, on the A44, is Batsford Arboretum, a 50-acre site of scenic walks and picnic areas open from April to October.

AA recommends:

Hotel: Manor House, High Street, 3-star, *tel.* 50501

Guesthouse: Moreton House, High Street, *tel.* 50747

The Devil's Chimney

The most famous landmark of the Cheltenham area is the pinnacle of rock jutting out of the scarp face of Leckhampton Hill, known locally and recorded officially on OS maps as the Devil's Chimney. It is some two miles south of Cheltenham and can be approached from the B4070. The hill was bought by Cheltenham District Council in 1929 and is now scheduled as a Site of Special Scientific Interest for its natural grasslands which make up the 400-acre common.

Leckhampton hilltop quarries had been worked extensively in the 18th century for the building of Georgian Cheltenham, and it was here on the highest range of the escarpment that the first Cotswold railway was attempted. Initially it was a pulley system to get the stone down to the main road and haul empty trucks up. Quarrying the hill was a thriving industry from Victorian times, first using horse-drawn trams, then engine-drawn rail trucks, until 1925.

The reasons for the quarrymen leaving the strangely-shaped column of stone intact are numerous, but the legend is the only one which has stood the test of two centuries.

The well-known saying 'As sure as God's in Gloucestershire' derived from the extraordinary number of abbeys and churches in the county. This annoyed the old Devil, so he hid on the edge of Leckhampton Hill and pulled out great rocks with his pitchfork to throw down on the monks and pilgrims that passed that way. His evil trick was reversed and the rocks fell on top of him, so he lives deep down in the Cotswold lime-stone below Dead Man's Quarry, the Chimney marking the spot.

The old GWR carriages and platform posters always used the Devil's Chimney to advertise the Cheltenham area. Scores of cyclists would swarm to the spot to have their photographs taken beside it, and the reckless who risked climbing it always left a coin on the cap as a token to Old Nick. The record was 13 people at any one time standing on the top. Climbing the Chimney is now strictly prohibited.

Erosion of this much-loved landmark put it in grave danger of collapse and created such a stir in the press that the Devil has recently had his Chimney repaired for some £25,000 — few mere mortals maintain such a costly chimney — but the Cotswolds would never be the same without it.

Nailsworth

Map Ref: 92ST8499

W H Davis, the super-tramp poet who made Nailsworth his last home, bade us make 'time to stand and stare' – and if one does, there is much to delight the eye and stir the senses.

Unpretentious and honestly workaday, Nailsworth does not conform to the typical Cotswold wool town picture. In the centre of the industrialised Stroud valley are the gaunt grey mills, their wheels now stilled, but brought back to life by the townsfolk, who have turned the old buildings into new enterprises.

What traditional Cotswold architecture there is stands out: gabled Stokes Croft with an oval window in each gable – a Nailsworth speciality – stands beside Chestnut Hill where formerly pack-horses climbed steeply up to the ancient trading routes. Humble weavers' cottages are still to be found along the roadside, and high above the valley, divorced from the clattering mills which built them, are the grand clothiers' houses.

A clock-tower marks the centre of this town of narrow steep streets, but it is the enormous copper kettle, which reputedly holds 82 gallons, hanging from a building in George Street, that strikes a more original note for it is one of the earliest forms of advertising.

Nonconformity flourished here in the aftermath of the Industrial Revolution, as evidenced by the meeting houses and chapels, all pre-dating the towerless church built five years after Nailsworth became a parish in 1895.

A mural enlivens the dreary Victorian church walls, including, within the spiritual theme, cameos of town life today – the brass band and the town crier, local views and wild flowers.

Artists, craftsmen and writers have always been attracted to this area: the original of John Halifax's mill is said to be Dunkirk Mills, the largest mill building in the district; and devotees of that enigmatic contemporary artist-writer Kit

Old mill buildings at Nailsworth, dating back to the 17th and 18th centuries.

Williams will recognise some of his spectacular scenes in the secret corners of the lovely countryside around.

AA recommends:
Guesthouse: Gables Private Hotel, Tiltups End, Bath Road, *tel.* 2265

Northleach

Map Ref: 89SP1114

Northleach was built as a market town in the 13th century, on a commercially strategic point on the Foss Way midway between Cirencester and Stow-on-the-Wold.

It was wool that made Northleach famous and its wealthy merchants built a magnificent church on their

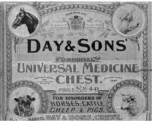

The interior of the lid of a veterinary surgeon's box, from the Countryside Collection at Northleach.

profits. The Church of St Peter and St Paul is one of Cotswold's outstanding 'wool' churches, and the likeness of the woolmen can be seen on a unique collection of memorial brasses. Notable among them are William Midwinter, whose transactions are detailed in the Cely papers; Thomas Busshe, Merchant of the Staple of Calais; John Taylor, with his 15 children, and John Fortey, with his initials in a medallion border.

The market-place stands east of the church and has many 16th- and 17th-century features in the old wool houses and inns lining the High Street. For years the little town was bedevilled by heavy traffic but is now bypassed, allowing visitors to, rather than through, it.

At the crossroads on the Foss Way is the Countryside Collection. A museum which has gained several awards since its opening, it makes splendid use of the old 'house of correction'. Built around 1789 by Sir Onesiphorus Paul, the building is a superb illustration of a prison of the period, and the important Lloyd-Baker agricultural collection is one of the best of its kind in the country.

AA recommends:
Garage: Clifford & Webb, Old Brewery Yard, *tel.* 306

Painswick

Map Ref: 86SO8609

'Painswick maidens shall be true Till there grows the hundredth yew.'

Legends abound at Painswick, and centred around the impressive colonnades of yew trees in the churchyard of St Mary's is the tradition that only 99 yews will grow at any one time – the Devil always killing off the 100th. So interwoven and divided have they become in 200 years that it is impossible to count the individual trees – but the exercise is a perennial favourite to send the children on.

The annual Clipping Ceremony (from the Saxon *ycleping*, meaning embracing) takes place on the Sunday on or following 19th September. The congregation of the open-air service join hands and encircle the church during the singing of the special Clipping Hymn. The children wear flowers in their hair and are rewarded by a coin and a Painswick bun.

The church was damaged by fire and vandalism during the Civil War, and cannon-ball marks are still visible below the clock-face on the tower. Around the church is a collection of Renaissance-style table tombs, designed and carved by a local family of masons, Joseph Bryan and his sons, John and Joseph. John's own tomb is inscribed 'carver'. The lych-gate was built with old belfry timbers and is decorated appropriately with bells and music. At the south-east entrance to the churchyard are the iron 'spectacle' stocks.

Painswick is a fine example of how size has nothing to do with stature, for this old market town is little larger than a village. Its earliest charter was granted in 1253 and New Street was set aside for development as the borough. Parallel to New Street, which was old in 1400, is Friday Street, speaking of an early market, and the delightful Tibbiwell with buildings full of character sloping steeply to the old mill valley.

Bisley Street was the original main street, and the oldest buildings, showing their ancient ties with the wool trade in a name or

Main picture: The famous clipped yew trees line the paths around Painswick churchyard with its renowned 17th- and 18th-century table tombs and iron stocks (inset).

pack-horse entrance, complete the square as the road divides eastward to Cheltenham, northward to Gloucester. Immediately south of the town are the mills on Painswick stream. Idyllic and tranquil, they hold the memory of a hard and busy life in their work-weary walls.

About a mile to the north is the beauty spot and viewpoint of Painswick Beacon, some 250 acres of common land on the escarpment, crossed with footpaths, a golf course and an Iron Age hill-fort, overlooking the Gloucester and Severn Vale.

AA recommends:
Hotel: Painswick, Kemps Lane, 3-star, *tel.* 812160

Prestbury

Map Ref: 87SO9723

The most haunted village of the Cotswolds is one of Prestbury's claims to fame.

It lies under the great bluff of Cleeve Hill: a pretty place so close to Cheltenham as to be counted mistakenly as a suburb, except that there is nothing suburban about Prestbury, for it has an old-world charm and identity of a long-established village in its own right.

Its roots go back beyond Domesday and its name means 'the priests' fortified place'. In 1249 Prestbury was granted a borough charter but did not expand into a prosperous market town owing to its close proximity to Cheltenham.

Cheltenham leased the steeplechase course at Prestbury Park in 1823 and has achieved fame ever since for the races under its own name. The legendary Fred Archer trained here and lived at the King's Arms, a pretty timbered inn. There are old buildings of thatch and stone and a church close to a stream.

North of the racecourse is Southam with its magnificent tithe barn in which an exhibition is held each July of the work of full-time Cotswold craftsmen.

The King's Arms Inn, Prestbury.

AA recommends:
Hotel: Rising Sun, Cleeve Hill, 2-star, *tel.* Bishop's Cleeve 2002
Guesthouse: Old Manor House, 43 Station Road, Bishop's Cleeve, *tel.* Bishop's Cleeve 4127
Garage: J & P Rose, Old Corn Mill, *tel.* 828411 (day) 610348 (night)

Prinknash Abbey

Map Ref: 86SO8713

'It stands on a glorious but impracticable hill, in the midst of a little forest of beech and commanding Elysium,' wrote Horace Walpole of Prinknash in 1774.

Prinknash Abbey, built in 1972 in glowing golden stone quarried at Guiting, stands in starkly simple modern style in the lush countryside beneath the west escarpment. It is in direct architectural contrast to the mellowed manor-house on the hill some half-a-mile away, which had served the Benedictine monks for almost half a century.

It was while digging the foundations for the new monastery that the rich beds of clay were discovered which started the famous Prinknash pottery. From the humble beginnings of making pots in a garden shed to modestly supplement the community's income, the Pottery has become the Abbey's major financial support, employing local people and exporting all over the world. Guided tours of the Pottery can be arranged. Incense and vestments, stained glass and ironwork are also made at Prinknash, and the crypt, consecrated as the Abbey church, is almost entirely furnished by the craft work of the monks.

Magnificent views over the Severn Vale can be seen from the Regency-walled monastery garden, which is open to the public.

Randwick

Map Ref: 78SO8206

The hills around are studded with barrows, long and round, and earthworks of the first settlers in this delightful wooded western edge. The valleys are dotted with mills and tiny villages which once eked out a meagre living in the cloth-making industry.

Randwick is just one of the many Stroud valley villages with a tale to tell of just how hard was the hard life: one Randwick son who became Regius Professor of Arabic at Oxford had, as a child, started weaving at 4 a.m. each day and did not finish until 10 p.m.

Poverty-stricken villagers welcomed the zealous arrival of nonconformist missionaries. George Whitefield attracted over 2000 to his service at Randwick and wrote that 'by taking down the window behind the pulpit' those in the churchyard could hear.

The old church on the hill attracts a crowd today to celebrate the ancient Randwick Wap. The first ceremony, held on the first Sunday in May, is the cheese-rolling. Three cheeses are carried to the church on flower-decked litters, blessed at a short service, rolled three times anti-clockwise round the church, then cut up and

The King's Men, a Bronze Age stone circle about 100ft in diameter, stand in upland country at the edge of the limestone belt overlooking Long Compton.

distributed by officers in costume.

The second part of the Wap, held on the second Saturday in May, is the mock mayor-making – a colourful and curious ceremony, which, like the cheese-rolling, dates back to medieval times and enlivens life in a small Cotswold village.

The Rissingtons

Map Ref: 91SP1917 to 91SP1921

Belonging to the north of the central wolds, on the rolling hillside and in the valleys inbetween, the Rissingtons put down their farming roots and came to terms with their windswept fieldscape 1000 years ago.

Great Rissington has two village greens: a three-cornered patch to which the main street runs uphill, and a square further to the north-west where the road divides. In the south-west corner is settled the group of church, rectory, manor and farm from which its history emanated.

Little Rissington is a mile away. The house and hangar complex on the high wold road was once famous as the Central Flying School – the Cotswold nest from where the Red Arrows aerobatic team flew. Many of the airmen came back to Little Rissington to be buried in the peaceful spot on the hill where the little Church of St Peter's stands in isolation apart from its village. Posies from the cottage gardens are laid by schoolchildren at an annual service.

Wyck Rissington another mile away lies at the foot of a steeply winding hill. The sweeping Cotswold stone roof of St Laurence is glimpsed from every bend. Full of character, the church can boast having had Gustav Holst as organist. His house faces the horse-grazed village green, which is the central point of this small farming community.

Robins Wood Hill Country Park

Map Ref: 86SO8415

The hill is one of Cotswold's outliers, detached from the main limestone mass. Since records of 1624 when it was Robinhoodes Hill, the hill became Robinswood, then Robin Hood's, as in the old ballad. A family of the name of Robins were tenants of the Matson manor in the 16th century and so it is reasonable to assume that they owned the ancient woodland, part of which still remains on the hill.

A unique feature of the hill is that it lies wholly within the city boundary of Gloucester. Owned by the City Council, 250 acres of Robins Wood is a country park with a warden and small information centre, two nature trails and a marked trail for horse-riding. There is a good variety of common flora and fauna and birds such as warblers and chiffchaffs.

The springs that for centuries supplied the city with water account for the number of ponds on the hill.

The reservoir is now a car park. The best approach to the Park is by Reservoir Road off the St Barnabus roundabout at the ring road.

On the west side of the hill is the Tuffley quarry, a Site of Special Scientific Interest for its Cotswold rock exposure and former base of the old George Whitfield brickworks.

The Matson side has the famous red well waters. Filtered through the iron stratum the red waters were revered for their purity, and within living memory people came to the well to bathe their eyes, convinced of the waters' curative properties.

Gloucester Country Club is the private owner of the remaining piece of the hill, on which there are two golf courses and one of the highest dry-ski slopes in England.

Matson manor-house was the headquarters of the Royalists during the siege of Gloucester, and sword cuts can still be seen on the window-sills. It was later the home of George Selwyn, famous for his deep slumbers in Parliament and quick wit when awake; he was a close friend of Sir Joshua Reynolds, who painted his portrait.

The Rollrights

Map Ref: 85SP2930 to 85SP3231

Legend has locked the Rollright Stones so firmly into the north-east Cotswold landscape that they carry their fabled names on the Ordnance Survey maps, an honour which their more famous Avebury cousins have not achieved.

Rollright, in a corrupt form of Roland the Brave – the legendary champion of Christianity – appears in Domesday, but the hoary old stones on the side of the road between Great and Little Rollright villages assumed their identity in medieval myth.

A king of old, setting out to conquer all England, strode up the hill and was halted by a witch who forecast that after taking seven long strides,

*'If Long Compton thou canst see,
King of England thou shalt be.'*

'Stick, stock, stone,' replied the aggressor, but as he stepped forward to survey his easily won kingdom his view of Long Compton was blocked by a long mound of earth. The witch turned the king and his men into stones and herself into an elder tree. The Whispering Knights, separated from the King's Men because they were whispering together plotting treason, also stand as monolithic reminders of a powerful past.

Long Compton, straggling along the A34 in its hollow below, has a fascinating lych-gate, with a room on top roofed with thatch.

Sezincote

Map Ref: 84SP1731

Sezincote is an experience, not a village. A victim of the early enclosure system, the village of Sezincote, which had supported a community of 12 plough teams at Domesday, had lost its church benefice to its neighbouring village of Longborough by 1750. Of its parish only a couple of farms remain. It is the house and garden which attract visitors to seek out this quiet place off the A424 Stow-to-Broadway road.

A cultural shock, sited as it is in Cotswold's central wolds, is the Indian-inspired mansion remodelled on an earlier building. Designed by Samuel Pepys Cockerell for his brother, Sir Charles, who made a fortune in the East India Company, Sezincote was visited by the Prince Regent in 1807 and gave him the inspiration for the Indianisation of the Brighton Pavilion.

To heighten the fantasy of the building and authenticate the colour of its material, the native stone was stained to impart a more Indian orange tone. The drive to the house is over an Indian-style bridge by Thomas Daniell, an expert artist in oriental design.

A temple-pool and shrine are at the head of the little valley, delightfully landscaped with the water-garden by Humphrey Repton, which attracts visitors throughout the year to its trees of unusual size.

The Shiptons

Map Ref: 88SP0318

Often it is only the melancholic bleat of sheep that breaks the silence of the Shiptons in the wilder wold country above the headlands of the Coln valley. The cluster of Shiptons on the high ridge off the A40 Cheltenham-to-Oxford road still accords closely with the sheep farmsteads of Saxon times.

Shipton and its twins, Oliffe and Solers, had a complicated division of lands owned by their respective patrons but were united as one parish in 1776; their former identities were distinguished by locating their churches.

St Oswald belongs to Shipton Oliffe, a small church with a beautiful bell turret made even prettier by tiny pinnacles. Inside are the remains of wall-paintings and early Norman work. The sanctuary is pannelled with oak from old pews discarded by its sister village Solers.

Shipton Solers also has a pretty church. It stands in a garen-like graveyard cleared of gravestones. One of its windows has a curious composition of a Cotswold house,

Cotswold Stone

The Cotswolds are part of a limestone belt which stretches from Dorset in the south to South Yorkshire in the north-east. In the Bath area the stone is a honey-gold colour. Further north at Painswick the white stone weathers to grey. At Chipping Campden and Broadway a deep golden colour is usual. The variety of colours results' from the varying quantities of iron present in the stone. On the high Cotswold hills the topsoil is usually only 6–12 inches deep and small loose limestone rocks are often seen on newly ploughed fields.

A few feet down stone can be quarried for wall building. Cotswold fields were first extensively walled in the 18th and 19th centuries, after the Enclosure Acts were introduced. Many walls are very old, but during a hard winter, frost may break up the stone and the walls will collapse. New stone walls can be seen along boundaries of roads such as the Northleach bypass. The stone is laid in courses and is protected on the top with *combers* (upright stones) which help to keep the wall dry. Years ago small farm cottages were built of this rough stone held together with mortar.

At a lower level in the quarry oolite freestone is found. When first quarried it is soft enough to be sculpted into window surrounds, mouldings and decorative motifs. Many examples of this beautiful work can be seen in the Cotswold wool churches — Fairford, Cirencester and Northleach are among the finest. Smooth-surfaced blocks called ashlar are cut for building. Good examples can be seen at Painswick, Chipping Campden and Minchinhampton.

Cotswold stone roofing slates are made from limestone blocks which split easily along the bedding plane when exposed to frost. Trimmed slates vary from 6–24 inches in depth and are graduated and overlapped from eave to ridge. The slates are held in place on the roof batten by oak pegs through a hole in the top of the slate. The different sizes have delightful names: Short Cock, Muffity, Short Bachelor, Short Wibbuts to mention just a few. Not many quarries are worked today, but all over the Cotswolds abandoned workings can be seen in large holes in fields near villages. The building stone for many Oxford colleges and St Paul's Cathedral in London came from Taynton near Burford.

Today, quarried stone is too expensive for most new houses, and coloured concrete or a mixture of sand and crushed stone is used to make blocks. Roofing slates are now moulded in concrete to look like stone. Most modern houses in the Cotswolds still follow the traditional Cotswold style of architecture.

A craft of a bygone age – dressing roofing slates. Repairs are now carried out by recycling slates from other houses or by using modern concrete copies.

corn sheaves and a ship. It may be that it is symbolic of Christianity sailing forth; if it was meant as a rebus, then the designer failed to understand the local dialect where 'ship' translates as 'sheep'.

There are yet two other Shiptons – Moyne is also in Gloucestershire, but not of Cotswold character; the other is Cotswold, but in Oxfordshire, anciently tied to Wychwood.

AA recommends:
Garage: Clifford & Webb, Old Brewery Yard, Northleach, *tel.* Northleach 306

Shipton-under-Wychwood

Map Ref: 91SP2717

Wychwood Forest, one of the five forests recorded in Domesday, gave the poachers on the Oxfordshire edge of the Cotswolds more venison in a week than a London alderman could afford in a year. Mid-Victorian enclosures finally reduced the vast forest to sparsely wooded outcrops, but the name remains.

Shipton – the sheep farmstead – was actually in the forest and a lively place when it was invaded by all and sundry for the great Wychwood Fair.

The focal point is the village green with the church at the far end sheltered by trees, but it is the sign of the Shaven Crown, swinging outside the honey-coloured inn on the roadside above the green, that catches the eye. Two projecting gabled wings flank a central hall, and lead-paned mullioned windows and a Tudor carriage entrance complete a pleasing picture. Few inns can match its record of serving travellers for six centuries, for it was first licensed in 1384. Its sign showing a monk's tonsure is possibly unique in all England and goes back to its monastic roots when it was a guesthouse for Bruern Abbey. In its long history it has served as medieval hospital, Tudor hunting lodge and a World War II army prison. Elizabeth I presented it to the parish on condition that it continued to be used as an inn.

At the old boundary where Shipton met with Widford and Fulbrook a lone oak tree was where two of the Dunsdon brothers were hanged in chains 200 years ago. Tom, Dick and Harry terrorised the highways with verve and flamboyance far beyond that of the fabled Dick Turpin.

The Slaughters

Map Ref: 90SP1523 to 90SP1622

The two small villages of Upper and Lower Slaughter stand on the little Eye stream which meets the Dikler to swell the waters of the Windrush. Slaughter is thought to have been the ancient name for either the stream itself or the slough (mire) caused by it.

Upper Slaughter was the home of a family called Slaughter in the 16th century, but the site has been inhabited since early times. A castle mound is just west of the river but has not been fully excavated. The village is completely unspoilt; an open square is bordered by cottages remodelled in 1906 in keeping with the Cotswold style and using local stone. The practical little bridges over the stream fringed with wild flower-filled grasses and the sounds of the countryside keep this small spot special.

Lower Slaughter downstream is the pretty sister. Here the water is a feature flowing broad and shallow between the neatly-mown grass banks.

There are many good houses with original features but much rebuilding of older cottages. Close regard has been paid to the overall unity because traditional stone has been used. The red brick-built corn mill with its tall chimney and water-wheel makes an attractive corner.

AA recommends:
Hotels: Lords of the Manor, Upper Slaughter, 3-star, Country House Hotel, *tel.* Cotswold 20243
Manor, Lower Slaughter, 3-star, Country House Hotel, *tel.* Cotswold 20456

Snowshill

Map Ref: 83SP0933

An isolated little hill village where winter snows lie longest is Snowshill, just east of the north scarpline and three miles south of busy Broadway. An unpretentious place with a history stretching back over 1000 years, the manor was given by the King of Mercia to the Abbey of Winchcombe and remained in monastic hands until the Dissolution when it was held by the Crown.

Snowshill manor-house first attracted attention in 1604. The story of how Ann Parsons was abducted from Elmley Castle to be married secretly at midnight on St Valentine's Eve has been well documented and gives an aura of romance to Ann's Room – an upper

The broad shallow stream flows past the old corn mill at Lower Slaughter.

part of the great hall.

Now owned by the National Trust, Snowshill Manor is a delightful combination: a traditional Cotswold manor-house, built of local stone dating back to around 1500; a terraced garden full of old-fashioned roses, shrubs and ponds; and a collection of which Queen Mary said that the most remarkable part was the collector. Charles Paget Wade amassed all kinds of curios of yesteryear in the manor-house, while he lived in a cottage where he refused any modern amenity and slept in a Tudor cupboard-bed.

Beyond the manor-house, the village, little more than a closely-knit clutch of old cottages and a tiny rebuilt church, edges the village green and spills down the hill, from which ancient tracks radiate to even smaller Laverton and Buckland in the wooded valley below.

AA recommends:
Self Catering: Oat Hill Farm Holidays, Snowshill, *tel.* Broadway 858758

A row of stone-built houses at Snowshill. The drystone wall, a typical Cotswold feature, is in good repair.

South Cerney and the Cotswold Water Park

Map Ref: 94SU0596

It lies south of Cirencester, on the Gloucestershire–Wiltshire border where the gentle hills of Cotswold country meet the water meadows of the Upper Thames valley. Cerney relates to the Churn stream on which the village stands, but the waters for which South Cerney is known are of its gravel pits.

Gravel has been extracted from the Upper Thames watershed since the 1920s but it was 40 years before plans were made to use the water-filled pits as a recreational resource. The south-eastern dip slope had none of the large open commons of the western scarp lands so the plan to designate a water park centred around South Cerney and reaching in a chain of lakes eastward to Lechlade was welcomed for inland water sports. By the end of the 1980s it is estimated that around 4000 acres of lakes will have been created. The two largest areas covering some 24 square miles are fully established south of South Cerney.

The Cotswold Water Park offers water sports, angling and sailing; to the east the Cotswold Leisure Centre at Somerford Keynes extends its facilities to windsurfing and guided tours around the lake reserves in a launch to observe the aquatic wildlife.

Lakeside walks and horse-riding along the disused rail line around South Cerney is in landscape typical of a lowland river valley with wetland flora and fauna – attracting nightingales in the summer, and heron, grebe, lapwing and warbler among the sedge and sallow, rush and willow. Walks along the towpath of the old Thames and Severn Canal radiate from and to Cerney.

The village itself retains its Cotswold heart, despite an expansion of new building. Unusual in having three manors, South Cerney also delights in unusual names: Bow-Wow is a pleasant walk close to the Old George Inn; Upper Up, now adjoining the village, is a reminder of the days when it was an outlying farming hamlet.

The village is on a long street plan; several houses in Silver Street date back to the 17th century, and Edwards College at the north end, built in Victoria's age as a home for clergy widows, is a fine composition of Tudor-Gothic style. A row of gabled cottages with mullioned windows are in Station Road. The church is large with a Norman tympanum and part of a fine wood crucifix, thought to be the earliest piece of wood-carving in the country.

The Cotswold Water Park attracts both human and wildfowl visitors, like the anglers (main picture) and the swan and Canada geese (inset).

Stanton

Map Ref: 82SP0634

The perfect Cotswold village – nothing has been allowed to spoil the simple classic lines of Stanton thanks to the foresight of the architect, Sir Philip Stott, who owned the estate from 1906 to 1937.

The buildings at Stanton owe much to the restoration work of Sir Philip Stott.

It lies about 3 miles south-west of Broadway and takes its name from *stan* (stone) farmstead. The long main street is lined with beautiful houses, and nowhere can the local stone and style be seen in such a homogeneous composition.

Tucked behind the village cross on its medieval base is St Michael's Church. It has the feel of age but there is much that is new. Sir

Ninian Comper 'signed' his work in one of the windows with a wild strawberry; it was he who reset the ancient glass of the east window, removed from Hailes Abbey and broken by Civil War soldiers who were locked in the church.

The steady tread of centuries has worn down the stone-flagged floor, and under the organ loft, also Comper's work, are medieval pews, their poppy heads gouged deep from the days when shepherds took their dogs to church and fastened them to the pew heads.

The road divides at the northern end, curving round a picturesque spot still known as Sheppey Corner from the age when flocks were shepherded off the hills to the manor's farm for shearing. Pointing the rise to the wooded scarp are the Mount Inn and a guild-house.

AA recommends:
Self Catering: Charity Cottage, Charity Farm, *tel.* 339

Stanway

Map Ref: 82SP0632

As with Stanton, Stanway takes its name from the local *stan* (stone), but here it is golden and deeply rich like a peach.

The village clusters close to its manor, Stanway House. The gatehouse, breathtakingly beautiful, was long supposed to have been by Inigo Jones, but is more likely to have been the work of Timothy Strong of Little Barrington. It is an architectural gem: the huge oak doors are carved with birds, and the scallop shell crest of the Tracys surmounts each of the three shaped gables above the roof line.

Stanway owes its precious cohesion of architectural unity and close-knit community living entirely to the manor. It is in the house, an exquisite Jacobean manor with its great hall lit by a window reaching almost to the eaves, its old library, romantic rooms, great passages and little lobbies, that the import of such an ancient lordship is realised. Its distinction lies in its domesticity, for it is, as shown, a typical squire's home furnished and furbished with the stuff of the families who have owned Stanway for centuries. Notable for having changed hands only once, other than by inheritance, in the last 1260 years (when it was bought at the Dissolution), it is unique in its rent audits at which its tenants appear in person.

The present heir to the estate, Lord Neidpath, opens the manor to the public on Tuesdays and Thursdays from June to August. Within the grounds and behind the church, is the magnificent tithe barn, built about 1370 in which the great and little tithes were stored for the Abbots of Tewkesbury, in whose charge the manor was at that

St Peter's Church next to the Gatehouse of Stanway House.

time. Today it serves as an incredibly beautiful hall in which music and art festivals are held, as well as the local flower show.

A thatched wooden cricket pavillion, set on staddle stones to keep it off the wetland field, was given to the village by Sir James Barrie and marks one end of the village. The war memorial at the other end is a splendid bronze sculpture of St George and the Dragon. The old vicarage, farm buildings and cottages set among ox-eye daisies and roses in bloom complete this old-world scene.

AA recommends:
Hotel: Buckland Manor, Buckland, I-rosette 3 red star, *tel.* Broadway 852626

Stow-on-the-Wold

Map Ref: 91SP1925

'Stow-on-the-Wold, where the wind blows cold,' runs the age-old jingle. Windswept throughout the centuries, Stow at nearly 800 feet, is the highest town in the Cotswolds.

Henry I granted borough status to Edwardstow. The receiving of the royal charter in 1107 is portrayed on the headstones of the market cross. St Edward is commemorated in the church dedication, an Elizabethan grammar school, an 18th-century house facing the cross and a Victorian hall in the centre of the market square, but has been dropped from the name of the town.

All Cotswold roads lead to Stow, they say; eight intersect here, which must make it one of the easiest places to find. On the path of the ancient ridgeway, the town centre is effectively bypassed by the Roman Foss Way, leaving it free of passing traffic. It is one of the few places without a museum or obvious tourist attraction. That tourists are attracted to Stow is reflected in the number of inns and tea-shops, pubs and hotels jostling for space around the square and down its narrow alleys, by its old almshouses and behind its ancient stocks.

Stow Fair, where some 20,000 sheep would change hands at a time, is still held twice a year but is now rooted firmly in the Cotswold calendar as Stow Horse Fair.

AA recommends:
Hotels: Old Farmhouse, Lower Swell (Im W B4068), 2-star, *tel.* 30232 Unicorn Crest, Sheep Street, 2-star, *tel.* 30257
Guesthouses: Limes, Evesham Road, *tel.* Cotswold 30034 Grapevine Hotel, Sheep Street, *tel.* Cotswold 30344

The old stocks in front of some renovated houses in Stow-on-the-Wold.

Stroud

Map Ref: 92SO8505

Most guidebooks gloss over Stroud, for it is the five valleys converging upon it and the old mills that punctuate its past and give character to its present that are the more attractive features.

Haphazardly built on steep hills of a spur above the River Frome, Stroud itself scores few marks for architectural merit, but it is a working town rather than a tourist haunt and so is remarkably free of quasi-quaint inns and antique shops. Its past is tucked away in a museum, housed in a Victorian building in Lansdown.

Stroud makes no effort to trade on its heritage as the west of England cloth-making centre. Stroudwater scarlet and Uley blue blazoned its fame abroad as military uniforms, but of the 150 mills which once worked the waters of the Frome and its tributaries only a couple are producing cloth today. Wealthy clothiers chose to build their grand houses on the outskirts of the town, but there is still character to be sought out in its steep and narrow streets.

The Shambles, the old meat market, and the Tudor Town Hall form a charming corner by the parish church, where the Women's Institute weekly stall with its jams and produce and an open-air market in Threadneedle Street bring colour to their respective patches.

The dignified building, boldly inscribed Stroud Subscription Rooms, accommodates the artistic and social life, while Stratford Park just outside the town offers sports and recreation at its 56-acre leisure centre.

A basket shop in the Shambles, Stroud. 'Shambles' were meat vendors' stalls.

AA recommends:
Hotel: Burleigh Court, Brimscombe (2½m SE off A419), 3-star, Country House Hotel, tel. Brimscombe 883804
Guesthouse: Downfield Private Hotel, Cainscross Road, tel. 4496
Garages: Auto Safety Centre, Cainscross Road, tel. 3527
Wicliffe Motor Company, Chestnut Lane, tel. 3671 (day) 2051 (night)

Sudeley Castle

Map Ref: 82SP0327

A castle has stood at Sudeley since the time of Ethelred the Unready; the present castle dates back to the mid-15th century when it was rebuilt by Ralph Boteler on the spoils of Henry V's wars.

On approaching the west arch the Portmare Tower on the right is named after the French admiral whom Boteler held prisoner there,

Sudeley Castle, near Winchcombe.

using his ransom money to pay for the extensions to the castle.

Queen Katherine Parr, widow of Henry VIII, brought her court to Sudeley on her marriage to Sir Thomas Seymour and is buried in the adjacent St Mary's Chapel. The chapel was desecrated by Cromwell's army, and the castle suffered extensive damage. The ruins of the Elizabethan banqueting hall stand testimony to the violence and scale of the Civil War which had made Sudeley 'the prize of all the buildings in those days'.

A thousand years of history are stored in this castle. Extensive areas of rooms and gardens are open to the public, filled with fascinating reminders of its chequered past. Europe's largest private collection of toys, arms and armour, antiques, fine paintings and an assemblage of Victoriana are the legacy of Emma Dent, a generous benefactor of Winchcombe, to whom the restoration of the castle is due. Falconry courses have just joined the ever increasing attractions of changing exhibitions, open-air theatre, Sealed Knot battles and holiday entertainment.

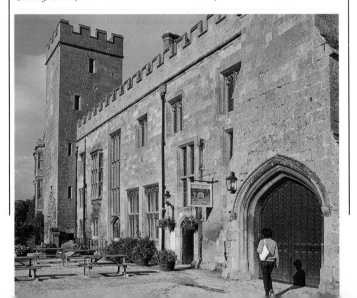

Tetbury

Map Ref: 92ST8993

'The design is entirely free from ostentation.' The description applies equally to the market town of Tetbury as it does to Highgrove, the most famous address in the British Isles.

Highgrove, the home of the Prince of Wales, a substantial country estate, was built in the 18th century for the Pauls, Huguenot immigrants who became prosperous clothiers. They gave to history Sir George Onesiphorus, the famous prison reformer, and Kitcat, the cricketer, who, in 1896, added 193 runs to the 301 of the legendary W G Grace, which is still the Gloucestershire record for the ninth wicket.

Careful park planning by a later owner ensured a clear view across the fields to see the slender spire of Tetbury's Gothic-styled church. St Mary's was rebuilt in 1781, using bits of medieval glass in its incredibly large windows. Narrow passages lead from the outer aisles to the old box pews, and there is a subtle epitaph to a local family – 'several of the Saunderses . . .

The airy interior of St Mary's, Tetbury.

particulars the Last Day will disclose'.

Tetbury's market-place adjoining the main thoroughfare was laid out by 1200 and all streets lead to it. At the north end is the Snooty Fox, a Jacobean-style building rebuilt last century to provide a ballroom on the first floor for the Beaufort Hunt. The Chipping, a lesser market, is beyond, with ancient remains of its brief period as a Cistercian priory. Chipping Steps are also of early medieval origin. There are many houses of some architectural merit in the town, but it is Gumstool Hill which is the focus of attention each year for this is where the celebrated Woolsack Races are held on the Monday of Spring Bank Holiday.

The agony of Gumstool Hill is a race of endurance and physical strength between two local teams, each competitor carrying a 65lb sack of wool from the Crown to the Royal Oak, down to the cattle-market and back up the hill, which in parts has a gradient of one in four. The fleeces arrive on horseback in keeping with the origins of the race of 400 years ago, when young drovers performed the feat to impress the young women of the town.

The Tetbury Festival, of which the Woolsack Races are a part, takes place in May, and stall-holders in medieval dress vie for attention with the morris dancers and mummers and the antics of the jester of Tetbury.

AA recommends:

Hotels: Calcot Manor, Calcot (3m NW), 3-star, Country House Hotel, *tel.* Leighterton 227

Snooty Fox, Market Place, 3-star, *tel.* 52436

Self Catering: Folly Farm, *tel.* 52358

Historic Houses and Gardens

The Cotswolds are rich in houses historically interesting for either their architecture, the role they played in some colourful event of the past, or for their inhabitants.

The strongest contender for the title of the oldest inhabited house in England is Horton Court in the south wolds. The Norman hall, now the north wing of the house, was built around 1140 — one of the few known domestic and unfortified houses of that date.

In the north wolds is Buckland Rectory, thought to be England's oldest and most complete medieval parsonage. Stone-built, with a most impressive hall with open timber roof, it dates back to the 15th century.

Chastleton House, near Stow-on-the-Wold, keeps a secret room in its early Jacobean walls, where a fugitive from the Battle of Worcester hid when Cromwell's soldiers stormed the house. Robert Catesby, a conspirator in the Gunpowder Plot, once owned the estate. Chavenage, near Tetbury, a fine Elizabethan house, has two bedrooms in the south-east wing named after Cromwell and Ireton, who slept there during one of the three sieges on nearby Beverstone Castle.

Owlpen Manor, near Dursley, is Tudor and exemplifies the typical Cotswold manorial grouping which is the nucleus of most villages.

Stanway House is an exquisite Jacobean house, a typical squire's residence, while Daneway House at Sapperton, dating back in part to

Kiftsgate Court near Mickleton. Part of the house and garden.

1250, was used by Gimson and the Barnsleys, who produced beautiful furniture in the Arts and Crafts revival in William Morris tradition.

Cotswold gardens range from the exotic collections of specialists to the cottage plots whose viewing is advertised only on a handwritten notice to raise funds for a village project.

Hidcote Manor garden was the first garden of outstanding merit to be presented to the National Trust, and Kiftsgate Court, its near neighbour, is renowned for its collection of roses and many unusual plants. A small plot in Leysbourne, off the High Street in Chipping Campden, is a newly-formed memorial garden to Ernest Wilson, whose world-wide travels introduced many of the now common species to the English garden.

The central Cotswolds has the knot and herb, and formal-style kitchen gardens within the overall garden of Barnsley House, designed by Rosemary Verey, the well-known writer and lecturer on English gardens.

At Bourton-on-the-Water two local men established world-famous collections in their own gardens: at Chardwar Manor the garden has become Birdland, and the whole village has been rebuilt, to scale, in the garden of the Old New Inn.

The south wolds has the folly garden at Stancombe Park, near Dursley, and the Italian garden of Westonbirt School, which was the 'nursery' for the great arboretum.

Viols from the Music Room at Snowshill Manor. In addition to the collection of musical instruments, there are toys, dolls' houses, perambulators, bicycles, armour, clocks and many other curiosities.

Tewkesbury

Map Ref: 80SO8932

An ancient and lovely town on the Avon, Tewkesbury belongs properly to the vale, but so dependent were the early fortunes of so many Cotswold manors on the monastic masters of Tewkesbury that they can scarcely be separated.

Tewkesbury Abbey was a powerful land-owner; its manor spread up and over the hills of the Cotswolds as far as Fairford in the south-eastern corner. The enormous tithe barn which can be seen today at Stanway gives some idea of the volume of great and little tithes stowed there for the abbot; and the fact that rustlers stole 1,000 head of the abbey flock from Stanway in 1340 illustrates the scale on which Tewkesbury Abbey farmed its sheep.

The town was already a royal borough by Domesday, and although it participated in the wool industry, it did not rise and fall on its fortunes as smaller hill towns did. Sited on the navigable Avon where it joins the Severn, Tewkesbury had the advantage of river transport years before roads were improved. This was the way the stone came for its mighty Norman abbey, brought from Normandy itself by sea and river.

The abbey is the central focus of the town. It was bought by the townsfolk at the Reformation for £453, and its sturdy tower still dominates the roofscape of the many timber-framed houses which are such an attractive feature of this riverside town.

The wide river and low-lying flood meadows resticted a sprawling growth and resulted in back-filling behind older buildings. The resultant narrow entrances have made Tewkesbury a place of secret

Tewkesbury Abbey, which dates back to Norman times.

alley-ways – an early Baptist chapel is tucked away in one, beyond the shadow of the great abbey.

Preservation of its historic past is strong: a unique terrace of houses, built about 1500, adjoins the abbey graveyard; and a delightful timber-framed house has been restored to house the works of John Moore, who captured the town and its characters in his amusing novels. The decisive Battle of Tewkesbury in the Wars of the Roses is re-enacted at festival time. The battlefield still bears the name of Bloody Meadow, and Gupshill Manor, which accommodated the royal party, still offers its services to today's travellers.

One of the oldest Mop Fairs in the country is held in October; the rights were granted by Elizabeth I and, although its purpose is no longer for the hiring of servants, it is the largest street fair to be held in Gloucestershire.

AA recommends:

Hotel: Tudor House, High Street, 2-star, *tel.* 297755

Self Catering: Auriol House, 124 High Street, *tel.* 298061

30 St Marys Lane, *tel.* Littlewick Green 5920

Guesthouses: Ancient Grudge Hotel, 15 High Street, *tel.* 292204

South End House, 67 Church Street, *tel.* 294097

Garages: Graham Wright Motors, Ashchurch Road, *tel.* 292398

Warners, Gloucester Road, *tel.* 293122

Acers at Westonbirt Arboretum, now managed by the Forestry Commission.

Westonbirt

Map Ref: 78ST8589

As the Cotswold hills flatten on the south-east side edging the Wiltshire plains, modest farmsteads give way to more palatial parkland and fox-hunting fields and coverts.

The village of Westonbirt, on the A433 some 3 miles south-west of Tetbury, was almost wholly rebuilt further west of its 14th-century church by the incredibly rich Victorian, R S Holford, to allow him the luxury of landscaped gardens on a lavish scale. The village, therefore, is interesting as a period-piece but does not follow the concept of traditional Cotswold building.

Westonbirt House was designed by Lewis Vulliamy, who had built Holford's Dorchester House (now the Dorchester Hotel) in Park Lane. Architecturally, Westonbirt – an Elizabethan-style palace – is an important survival. It is now a fashionable girl's school.

Its formal Italian-style garden, terraced with rustic walks and lake and filled with many rare and exotic shrubs, is sometimes open to the public in the summer. But the legacy of Holford's passion for gardens by the acre is the arboretum.

Westonbirt Arboretum is the

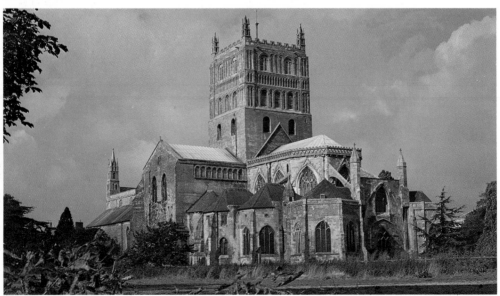

largest in the country. A magnificent landscaped collection of trees and shrubs covering some 600 acres, its has been managed by the Forestry Commission since 1956 and is open to the public from 10 a.m. until dusk all the year round. An honesty box by the gazebo allows for appreciative donations. Springtime at Westonbirt means rhododendrons and azaleas in glorious profusion and autumn is ablaze with fiery maples.

The visitors' centre, open from March to November, has a continuous audio-visual presentation of the arboretum, its management and objectives, and a brief history of the Holford family.

Winchcombe

Map Ref: 82SP0228

Sheltered under the bluff of the north-west hills, the small town of Winchcombe settled in its winding combe long ago in Saxon times. Capital of what was then a separate shire, Winchcombe was the seat of Mercian royalty. Offa built a nunnery here in 790; Kenulf, his successor, founded an abbey in 811 and Kenulf's son, Kenelm, left it a legacy of legend.

Miracles wrought in the name of the young murdered Kenelm made Winchcombe a place of pilgramage and its abbey rich and powerful. Of the abbey nothing remains today, but St Peter's Church was built close by as a joint venture between the abbot, who was responsible for the chancel, and Sir Ralph Boteler of Sudeley, who built the nave on behalf of the parish.

After the Dissolution the town looked to the land again and began to grow tobacco. Samuel Pepys wrote of the troops being sent 'to spoil the crop', Parliament being more interested in developing its interests in the newly-established outpost of Virginia than in supporting small local economy.

The past has left to Winchcombe some fine old inns, such as the

George, where, carved on the doorway, are the initials of Richard Kidderminster, the 16th-century abbot who raised the status of the abbey to 'equal a little university'.

Tudor buildings survive in Hailes Street leading downhill and northward. On the corner of North Street hefty timber stocks stand outside the Folk Museum, which has a fine collection of international police memorabilia and is the tourist information centre.

Abbey Terrace angles off south-westward, the church with magnificently grotesque gargoyles dominating the junction with Gloucester Street. Vineyard Street, with rustic porched cottages and pollarded trees, slopes steeply off southward to cross the Isbourne in which the town scolds were once ducked. Further on lies Sudeley Castle.

A strenuous climb from here over Humblebee How goes to Belas Knap. Car travellers can get within ¾ mile of the ancient long barrow by continuing along Gloucester Street, passing the charming Old Corner Cupboard Inn, to follow the well-signposted route up Corndean Lane.

Belas Knap is the finest example of a false-entrance long barrow on the Cotswolds. Constructed with huge slabs of the oolite limestone to form its burial chambers, it is the revetment walls of the thin ragstone which attract attention. For here high up on the westerly plateau, laid completely without mortar, the dry-stone walling stands as testimony to the Cotsaller's skill at handling his native stone 4,000 years ago.

AA recommends:

Self Catering: Cockbury Court Cottages, *tel.* Bishop's Cleeve 4153
The Malt House, Corner Cupboard Inn, *tel.* 602303
Garage: Winchcombe Motors, Broadway Road, *tel.* 603299 (day) Evesham 881761 (night)

Climbers round porches and well-kept flowerbeds give a picture-book charm to this row of cottages in Winchcombe.

Witney

Map Ref: 79SP3509

Weaving the wool grown on the Cotswolds was not confined to its hill settlements. In the flat plain across the Windrush in Oxfordshire, Witney grew up on the weaving industry. A 'fuller's isle' was recorded at Witney in an Anglo-Saxon charter, and there were two fulling mills by 1223.

Developing from the cloth-making industry, blankets were being made in Witney in the 16th century; plentiful supplies of local wool and the purity of the Windrush waters attracted financial support from a group of wealthy weavers who obtained the Charter for the Company of Blanket Weavers in 1711 and built Blanket Hall in 1721.

Flower-bedecked pub in Witney.

Witney blankets achieved fame early – coveted by the American Red Indians 300 years ago, they still find a ready export and home market. Industrial technology has drastically changed the working processes in the factories, and other industries attracted to the town have wrought changes in its street plans and facilities.

The low buildings of the old factories, a wide green and a handful of older houses make a pleasant background to its modern urban face. Even older memories are stirred at the September fair, still known as Witney Feast, and tangible reminders of the past are preserved along the road at Cogges Farm Museum.

Devoted to country life and the preservation of agricultural history, displays are housed in farm buildings and the old manor-house. There is nothing static about Cogges; changing exhibitions, country fairs and demonstrations of the many facets of rural life, from sheep-dog competitions to butter-making, keep alive the skills and crafts of yesteryear.

AA recommends:

Hotel: Old Swan, Minster Lovell, 2-star, *tel.* 75614
Guesthouse: Hill Grove, Minster Lovell (farmhouse), *tel.* 3120
Garage: M A Wilkins, 1A Bridge Street, *tel.* 3361

Wotton-under-Edge

Map Ref: 78ST7593

The old town of Wotton suffered total destruction in King John's reign when it was put to the torch by mercenaries taking their revenge on the Berkeley estates. Rebuilt, it regained its borough status in 1253, and its tenured plots, each of one-third of an acre, were let for a shilling a year.

The powerful Berkeley family lived a few miles away from the town, and Thomas Lord Berkeley is buried in Wotton church. Katherine Lady Berkeley built a house in 1384 for a master and two poor boys, on the principles of Winchester, so giving Wotton the distinction of having the first school to be founded by a woman. The present school, far removed from those humble beginnings of 600 years ago, still bears the name of that lady of foresight.

The Bluecoat School, founded in 1715, in in Culverhay. Isaac Pitman was the first master of the British School, on the corner of Bear Lane, and perfected his *Stenographic*

Wotton-under-Edge church.

Shorthand while there, teaching it first as a voluntary subject to the boys.

The High Street continues into Long Street, the Tolsey House on the corner making a prominent feature with its copper dragon weather-vane. Long Street leads to Church Street. The 17th-century almshouses and chapel – a bequest of Hugh Perry, who became Sheriff of London in 1632 – are beautiful gabled buildings and much admired for their architectural planning in a market town which has rebuilt according to its needs.

AA recommends:

Guesthouse: Under the Hill House, Adey's Lane (farmhouse), *tel.* Dursley 842557

Garage: Wotton Motor Centre, Wotton-under-Edge, *tel.* Dursley 842240 (day) Dursley 843334 (night)

Cotswold Ale and Gloucester Cheese

B rewhouses are still to be spotted at the back of some of the older houses where the ales and wines were made for large households before tea and coffee became popular and more readily available. As hard to find are the old cider presses and cheese rooms, but they do exist, mainly on private farms.

The Cotswolds was once a successful wine-growing area and vineyards were established on the gentler hill slopes around the ancient monasteries. A newly-planted vineyard at Charlton Court near Tetbury is just producing its first white wine of modern times.

Cider was brewed for strictly local consumption, and the farm labourers quaffed millions of gallons in the Cotswold harvest fields. When Gimson and the Barnsley brothers

Donnington Brewery. Taking a dip to check the quantity and gravity of the brew.

were at Daneway House they made 2,000 gallons in one year from their apple crop for sale to the Sapperton farmers. Pears grew better in the vale, and one tree, known as the Great Westbury Pear, once covered one-and-a-half acres; its branches rooted to form another tree.

Cider is made today at Smith's Fruit Farm at Chipping Campden, and for a few weeks each year the intoxicating aroma of crushed and fermented apples spices the crisp autumn air.

The two smallest breweries in England are in the Cotswolds. Arkell's established their brewery at Donnington Mill in 1865. From this picturesque spot 17 public houses are served with traditional ale with a unique local flavour. Smaller still and a newer venture is the revitalising of the old brewing skills in the Cellar Brewery at Cirencester.

Dairy farming has developed on the Cotswolds over the years and the only farm which makes yoghurt in Gloucestershire is at Perrotts Brook, near Cirencester. Several tons of yoghurt and gallons of lush dairy cream serve local shops and those as far afield as London and the Welsh border.

Only one registered cheesemaker is left in Gloucestershire, a county which was producing over 1,000 tons of cheese a year last century. Keeping the tradition alive by taking his cheese to sell at the market-place, Charles Martell is to be found at Cirencester market with a range of over 60 varieties of home-made cheese. From the Martell's small dairy comes the Double and Single Gloucester — the rich cheese made from the now rare breed Old Gloucestershire cattle. Charles Martell is the only cheesemaker in the world making this cheese in the traditional manner.

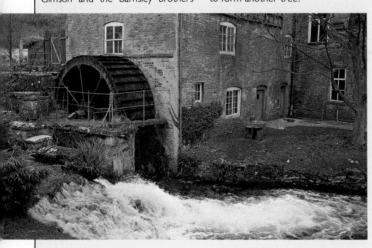

Donnington Mill, just north of Stow-on-the-Wold, now houses Donnington Brewery, suppliers of traditional ales to pubs in the area.

Directory

ANGLING

Day tickets may be purchased for coarse and game fishing at a number of Cotswold locations. Rod licences are available from Thames Water Authority while further details of Cotswold Water Park lakes may be obtained from Keynes Park Country Park, Somerford Keynes *tel* Cirencester (0285) 861459.

ANTIQUES

Picturesque Cotswold towns and villages provide an ideal setting for a flourishing antique trade, with a variety of shops and markets catering for all tastes. **Stow-on-the-Wold** is recognised as the antiques centre of the Cotswolds with a fine range of shops in the market square, while places such as **Broadway, Moreton-in-Marsh, Chipping Campden, Nailsworth** and **Tetbury** are also noted centres. **Cheltenham** too has a wide variety of shops and an Antique and Craft Market on Saturdays (Winchcombe Street), while in **Gloucester** one of the restored warehouses at the docks has been converted to an Antiques Centre with 47 individual shops on four floors.

ARCHAEOLOGY

There is much to fascinate the historian and archaeologist in the Cotswolds; in addition to the museums there are a variety of interesting sites to visit and explore.

Belas Knap: Two miles south-west of Winchcombe this Bronze Age chambered burial mound dates back some 4000 years. When excavated in 1863, 38 skeletons were found in six separate chambers.

Hetty Pegler's Tump: A mile north of Uley, this famous tumulus is named after a local landowner. *Tump* is also used locally to refer to a small hill or mound.

Uley Bury: One of the finest examples of an Iron Age hill-fort situated on the scarp edge just north of Uley, 800 feet above sea level. A walk around the ramparts yields panoramic views over the Severn Vale.

Crickley Hill: Neolithic settlements and an Iron Age hill-fort are still being excavated in this Country Park just south of Cheltenham. The digs can be visited during July and August, with guided tours held annually one weekend in August.

Chedworth Roman Villa: Constructed between AD 180–350 this fine example of a villa with mosaic floors and 32 rooms around a courtyard was first discovered in 1864. Now owned by the National Trust it is open between March and October (Tuesday–Sunday) and Bank Holiday Mondays.

CRAFTS

An abundance of craft workshops, markets and galleries ensures that wherever you go in the Cotswolds there is a chance of finding a gift of local origin and perhaps of seeing it being made.

Bourton-on-the-Water: This famous Cotswold village has a variety of gift shops and other features of interest. The *Cotswold Perfumery* includes a laboratory where visitors may test the products, an exhibition of perfume manufacture and shop (open daily). The *Chestnut Gallery* in the High Street has a large selection of British crafts and occasional exhibitions (open daily).

Chipping Campden: The *Campden Pottery* in the High Street has a workshop and showroom full of hand-thrown pottery (open daily except winter Sundays). *Campden Weavers* at 16 Lower High Street, Leasebourne, specialises in local weaving and has a showroom open daily.

Cirencester: Recent developments have enabled a fine range of workshops to be established. In the old brewery in Cricklade Street the *Cirencester Workshops* house a variety of crafts and exhibitions and incorporate 12 independent workshops (open Monday to Saturday all year). A weekly craft market is held each Saturday (except January and February) at the *Corn Hall* and features such crafts as woodwork, jewellery, pottery and silk-screen printing. Visitors may practise *brass-rubbing* on replica church brasses by calling at the Corn Hall by the market-place (Mondays to Fridays).

Filkins: On the A361 between Burford and Lechlade is the *Cotswold Woollen Weavers* where a magnificent 18th-century barn houses a working weaving mill with traditional machinery and an exhibition tracing the history of wool and weaving in the Cotswolds. Rugs, clothes and material are woven here and the centre includes a coffee shop and art gallery. Open daily except Sunday mornings.

Painswick: An annual festival in the town in August includes exhibitions of arts and crafts. Not far away is *Prinknash Abbey* where the Benedictine monks and other craftsmen produce a distinctive range of pottery (open daily).

Stinchcombe: Just a little way from this village on the western edge of the Cotswolds is the *Cider Mill Gallery* at Blanchworth Farm. The craft shop, art gallery and traditional cider-making with a horse-drawn mill and press have attracted a great deal of attention from visitors to the area.

Crushing the apples using old-fashioned horsepower at the Cider Mill Gallery.

CALENDAR OF EVENTS

March
Cheltenham Gold Cup. One of the greatest races in the National Hunt season.

April
St George's Day Mummers and Morris Dancers, Gloucester. A celebration of the feast day held in the centre of town.

May
Woolsack Races and Fayre, Tetbury. Fairs, markets and exhibitions as well as the traditional races with competitors carrying 50lb sacks of wool. *Cheese-rolling* takes place at Cooper's Hill (late May Bank Holiday) when Double Gloucesters are chased down the hill by local youths, the winner taking home the cheese.

June
Dover's Games at Dover's Hill, Chipping Campden. One of the oldest customs, these Olympic games were begun in the 17th century with such entertaining sports as shin-kicking.

July
Cheltenham Festival of Music with many leading performers from around the world. *Stow Horse Fair.*

August
Cranham Feast. A traditional deer and ox roast on the beautiful common at Cranham.

September
Clipping the Church, Painswick. A festival of singing and dancing in the churchyard, famous for its table tombs and yew trees. Sunday nearest 19th. *Moreton-in-Marsh Agricultural Show* – the leading show of the Cotswolds.

October
Cheltenham Festival of Literature – a week of literary events. *Cirencester Mop Fair* – one of many such events traditionally held when labour was hired for the year ahead. Two successive Mondays near 11th. *Stow Horse Fair* – the second of the year's traditional fairs at Stow-on-the-Wold.

GARDENS

In this most picturesque part of England we find some of the most attractive gardens and arboreta in the country. Of all shapes, sizes and styles they range from castles to manors to cottage gardens. It is impossible to provide a full catalogue of places to visit and further details may be found in the National Garden Scheme's booklets, available locally.

Batsford Park Arboretum: Two miles west of Moreton-in-Marsh the Park was originally landscaped by Lord Redesdale in the mid-19th century. Amongst the fine collection of over 1,000 different trees and shrubs is a number of oriental statues and a replica of a Chinese temple. Open daily April to October.

Buscot House and Park: On the A417 south-west of Lechlade the house was built in 1780 and is set on higher ground surrounded by a landscaped garden including a formal Italianate water garden. Open Wednesday to Friday, April to September.

Cirencester Park: On the outskirts of Cirencester some 3,000 acres of parkland dating from the 18th century are open for public enjoyment. Broad avenues, woodland and pasture provide pleasant surroundings for quiet walks.

Dyrham Park: Seven miles north of Bath, Dyrham House, built about 1700, belongs to the National Trust and the surrounding parkland contains one of the country's oldest herds of fallow deer.

Hidcote Manor: One of the finest 20th-century gardens now owned by the National Trust, Hidcote Manor's 300 acres include a series of formal gardens, many enclosed by superb hedges and containing many unusual plants. Open daily except Tuesdays and Fridays, April to October.

Main picture: Steeplechasers tackle a fence at Cheltenham. Above top: Deer roasting at the Cranham Feast. Above: Prospective buyers at Stow Horse Fair.

Kiftsgate Court: Near the village of Mickleton this attractive garden commands superb views over the countryside and contains many unusual trees and flowers. Open Wednesdays, Thursdays and Sundays, April to September.

Sezincote Garden: Near Bourton-on-the-Hill this is a garden in the grand style, landscaped by Daniell and Repton after oriental themes and surrounding the 18th-century Sezincote House. Garden open (not the house) Thursdays, Fridays and Bank Holiday afternoons except December.

Snowshill Manor: Another attractive North Cotswold garden surrounds this National Trust property in the delightful village of Snowshill, near Broadway. Open Wednesday to Sunday, May to October; weekends only April and October; Bank Holidays.

Sudeley Castle: On the outskirts of Winchcombe Sudeley Castle is rich in Tudor history. The interest of the castle itself is complemented by the extensive gardens and attractions such as falconry displays. Open April to October.

Westonbirt Arboretum: This famous arboretum near Tetbury is cared for by the Forestry Commission. Begun in the early 19th century by Robert Holford, the collection now extends over 1,000 acres. Particular attractions are the autumn colours and spring azaleas and rhododendrons. Open daily.

GOLF

Cirencester Golf Club, Bagendon, *tel* Cirencester (0285) 2465. 18 hole course in attractive Cotswold valley.

Cotswold Hills Golf Club, Ullenwood, Cheltenham, *tel* Cheltenham (0242) 515264. 18 hole gently undulating course.

Painswick Golf Club, near Stroud, *tel* Painswick (0452) 812180. 18 hole course near Painswick Beacon, one of the best viewpoints in the Cotswolds.

Stinchcombe Hill Golf Club, near Dursley, *tel* Dursley (0453) 2015. 18 hole course on hill-top location commanding panoramic views of the Cotswolds, the River Severn and the Welsh hills.

Broadway Golf Club, Willersey Hill, Broadway, *tel* Broadway (0386) 853683. 18 hole course 900 feet above sea level with extensive views.

MARKETS
Markets are a traditional feature of many Cotswold towns, some of them dating back hundreds of years.
Cheltenham   *Thursdays* *(Market Street) and Saturdays (Winchcombe Street)*

Chipping Norton	*Wednesdays*
Cirencester	*Mondays and Fridays*
Gloucester	*Saturdays*
Moreton-in-Marsh	*Tuesdays*
Stroud	*Saturdays*

MUSEUMS
The rich history of the Cotswolds is reflected in the number and variety of its attractive museums located in many centres across the area.

Bibury *Arlington Mill Museum.* This 17th-century mill is now a farm museum exhibiting a range of implements and machinery. Open daily in summer; weekends in winter.

Cheltenham Among the museums and galleries are the *Art Gallery and Museum* in Clarence Street (open Monday to Saturday), the *Gustav Holst Museum* in Clarence Road (open Tuesday and Friday afternoons and Saturdays) and the *Pittville Pump Room Museum* with its exhibitions of costumes and jewellery (open daily except Mondays, closed Sundays November to March).

Burford *Tolsey House Museum.* This museum contains the town's seals and charters from the 13th century. Open daily, Easter to September.

Chipping Campden *Woolstaplers Hall Museum.* Housed in one of the town's oldest buildings (1340), the museum contains a fine array of county bygones (including mantraps). Open daily April to September, weekends October.

Cirencester *Corinium Museum.* This excellent museum houses one of the finest collections of Roman antiquities in the country and includes reconstructions of a Roman kitchen, dining room and mosaic craftsmen's workshop (open daily except winter Mondays).

Gloucester The *City Museum and Art Gallery* in Brunswick Road includes historical and natural history displays, while the *Folk Museum* in Westgate Street is in three half-timbered Tudor houses and demonstrates agriculture, industries and crafts of the county. Both open daily except Sundays.

Kemble *Smerrill Farm Museum.* On the A429 this collection traces the agricultural history of the area. Open daily.

Northleach *Cotswold Countryside Collection.* Recently established in the 18th-century police station and prison, this museum of rural life exhibits farm tools, machinery and wagons and contains the Lloyd Baker Collection of agricultural history. Open daily April to October.

Stroud *Stroud and District Museum* at Lansdown. This museum contains exhibits of geology, archaeology and local crafts. Open daily except Sundays.

RIDING AND TREKKING
Camp Riding Centre, Camp, Nr Stroud, Glos., *tel* Miserden (028 582) 219.

Long Distance Riding Centre, Mead House, Rissington Road, Bourton-on-the-Water, Glos., *tel* Cotswold (0451) 21101.

South Cerney Riding School, Cerney Wick Farm, Cerney Wick, Cirencester, *tel* Swindon (0793) 750151 – hacking, tuition and accommodation.

Southam Riding School, Southam De La Bere, Prestbury, Cheltenham, *tel* Cheltenham (0242) 42194.

Talland School of Equitation, Church Farm, Siddington, Cirencester, *tel* Cirencester (0285) 2318/2437.

THEATRE
Cheltenham is the cultural centre for the Cotswolds and frequent theatrical productions at the **Cheltenham Playhouse** and **Everyman Theatre** attract large audiences. Both **Sudeley Castle** and **Hidcote Manor** provide magical settings for open-air performances in July and August.

WATER SPORTS
The **Cotswold Water Park** offers a variety of sports activities including sailing, water-skiing and wind-surfing. Details available from Keynes Park, Somerford Keynes, *tel* Cirencester (0285) 861459.

WILDLIFE AND FARMS
Birdland A collection of some 600 different species of birds in over 3 acres of parkland at Bourton-on-the-Water. Open daily.

Cotswold Farm Park The Rare Breeds Survival Centre near Guiting Power maintains a collection of rare farm animals. Open daily May to September.

Cotswold Wildlife Park 200 acres of gardens and woodland at Burford with a collection of animals from around the world. Other features include a narrow-gauge railway and butterfly house. Open daily.

Folly Farm Two miles from Bourton-on-the-Water the farm has an outstanding collection of rare and unusual ducks, geese and poultry. Open daily.

Trout Farms Situated in villages such as **Bibury, Alderley** and **Bourton-on-the-Water.** Visitors may walk around the farms and purchase fresh fish.

COTSWOLDS

Atlas

The following pages contain a legend, key map and atlas of the Cotswolds, three circular motor tours and sixteen planned walks in the Cotswolds countryside.

Above: The north Cotswold village of Saintbury descends the slope below its medieval church.

Cotswolds Legend

TOURIST INFORMATION (All Scales)

𝖷 𝖷	Camp Site		Nature reserve
	Caravan Site	☆	Other tourist feature
🅸 🅸	Information Centre		Preserved railway
🅿 🅿	Parking Facilities		Racecourse
	Viewpoint		Wildlife park
🗶 🗶	Picnic site		Museum
	Golf course or links		Nature or forest trail
	Castle	⋒	Ancient monument
	Cave		Places of interest
	Country park	❛❜	Telephones: public or motoring organisations
	Garden		Public Convenience
	Historic house	▲	Youth Hostel

◆—◆ Waymarked Path / Long Distance Path

ORIENTATION

True North
At the centre of the area is 4½'W of Grid North

Magnetic North
At the centre of the area is about 6° W of Grid North in 1986 decreasing by about ½° in three years

GRID REFERENCE SYSTEM

The map references used in this book are based on the Ordnance Survey National Grid, correct to within 1000 metres. They comprise two letters and four figures, and are preceded by the atlas page number.

Thus the reference for Cirencester appears 93 SP 0201

93 is the atlas page number

SP identifies the major (100km) grid square concerned (see diag)

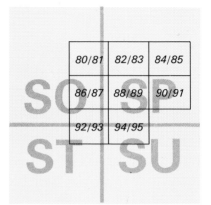

0201 locates the lower left-hand corner of the kilometre grid square in which Cirencester appears

02 can be found along the bottom edge of the page, reading W to E

01 can be found along the right hand side of the page, reading S to N

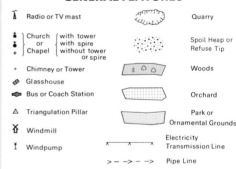

ATLAS 1: 63,360 or 1" to 1 MILE

ROADS & PATHS Not necessarily rights of way

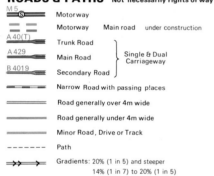

M 5	Motorway
	Motorway Main road under construction
A 40(T)	Trunk Road
A 429	Main Road } Single & Dual Carriageway
B 4019	Secondary Road }
	Narrow Road with passing places
	Road generally over 4m wide
	Road generally under 4m wide
	Minor Road, Drive or Track
	Path
	Gradients: 20% (1 in 5) and steeper 14% (1 in 7) to 20% (1 in 5)

GENERAL FEATURES

	Radio or TV mast		Quarry
	Church or Chapel {with tower / with spire / without tower or spire}		Spoil Heap or Refuse Tip
∘	Chimney or Tower		Woods
	Glasshouse		Orchard
	Bus or Coach Station		Park or Ornamental Grounds
△	Triangulation Pillar		
	Windmill		Electricity Transmission Line
	Windpump	>- -> - ->	Pipe Line

RAILWAYS

	Multiple or Single Track
	Narrow Gauge Track
	Bridges. Footbridge
	Tunnel. Cutting

	Freight Line, Siding or Tramway
	Station (a) principal (b) closed to passengers
	Level crossing
	Viaduct. Embankment

ABBREVIATIONS

P	Post Office
PH	Public House
MP	Mile Post
MS	Mile Stone
LDP	Long Distance Path
CH	Club House
TH	Town Hall, Guildhall or equivalent
PC	Public Convenience (in rural areas)

WATER FEATURES

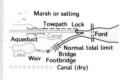

Marsh or salting
Towpath Lock
Aqueduct   Canal   Ford
Lake Weir Normal tidal limit
Bridge Footbridge
Canal (dry)

BOUNDARIES

+—+—	National	.—.—.—	County
	National Park	+ + + +	District
NT	National Trust	NT always open NT opening restricted	
FC	Forestry Commission	Pedestrians only – observe local signs	

ANTIQUITIES

VILLA	Roman	Castle	Non-Roman
⚔	Battlefield (with date)		
☆	Tumulus		
+	Site of Antiquity		

PUBLIC RIGHTS OF WAY

·············	Footpath	-·-·-·-·-	Road used as a Public Path
---------	Bridleway	+-+-+-+-	By-way open to all traffic

Public rights of way indicated by these symbols have been derived from Definitive Maps as amended by later enactments or instruments held by Ordnance Survey on 1st August 1985 and are shown subject to the limitations imposed by the scale of mapping. Later information may be obtained from the appropriate County Council.

The representation in this atlas of any other road track or path is no evidence of the existence of a right of way.

Danger Area   MOD Ranges in the area. Danger! Observe warning notices

HEIGHTS & ROCK FEATURES

outcrop   cliff   scree

Contours are at 10 metres vertical interval

·144 Heights are to the nearest metre above mean sea level

Heights shown close to a triangulation pillar refer to the station height at ground level and not necessarily to the summit.

TOURS 1:250,000 or ¼"to 1 MILE

ROADS   Not necessarily rights of way

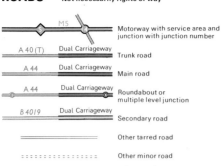

Motorway with service area and junction with junction number

A 40 (T)   Dual Carriageway   Trunk road

A 44   Dual Carriageway   Main road

A 44   Dual Carriageway   Roundabout or multiple level junction

B 4019   Dual Carriageway   Secondary road

Other tarred road

Other minor road

Gradient 1 in 7 and steeper

RAILWAYS

Road crossing under or over standard gauge track

Level crossing

Station

Narrow gauge track

WATER FEATURES

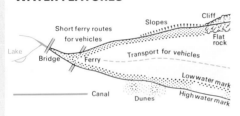

ANTIQUITIES

⚬ Native fortress

------ Roman road (course of)

Castle · Other antiquities

CANOVIVM · Roman antiquity

GENERAL FEATURES

Buildings

Wood

ℓ ℓ Telephones: public or motoring organisations

⊕ Civil aerodrome (with custom facilities)

Ⅹ Radio or TV mast

Ⅱ Lighthouse

RELIEF

Feet	Metres	
		.274 Heights in feet above mean sea level
3000	914	
2000	610	
1400	427	Contours at 200 ft intervals
1000	305	
600	183	
200	61	
0	0	To convert feet to metres multiply by 0.3048

WALKS 1:25,000 or 2½"to 1 MILE

ROADS AND PATHS Not necessarily rights of way

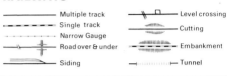

M5   Motorway

A 40 (T)   Trunk road

A 417   Main road

B 4040   Secondary road

A 417   Dual carriageway

} Narrow roads with passing places are annotated

Road generally over 4m wide

Road generally under 4m wide

Other road, drive or track   .... Path

RAILWAYS

Multiple track   Level crossing

Single track   Cutting

Narrow Gauge

Road over & under   Embankment

Siding   Tunnel

GENERAL FEATURES

Church } with tower
or } with spire
Chapel } without tower or spire

Electricity transmission line
pylon pole

⚬ Gravel pit   NT National Trust always open

Sand pit   NT National Trust opening restricted

Chalk pit, clay pit or quarry   FC Forestry Commission pedestrians only (observe local signs)

Refuse or slag heap   National Park

HEIGHTS AND ROCK FEATURES

Contours are at 5 metres vertical interval

50 ·   Determined { ground survey
285 ·   by { air survey

Surface heights are to the nearest metre above mean sea level. Heights shown close to a triangulation pillar refer to the station height at ground level and not necessarily to the summit.

Vertical Face

Loose rock   Boulders   Outcrop   Scree

75
60
50

PUBLIC RIGHTS OF WAY

Public rights of way shown on this Atlas may not be evident on the ground.

} Public Paths { Footpath
Bridleway

+ + + + +   By-way open to all traffic

Road used as a public path

Public rights of way indicated by these symbols have been derived from Definitive Maps as amended by later enactments or instruments held by Ordnance Survey between 1st September 1972 and 1st October 1984 and are shown subject to the limitations imposed by the scale of mapping.
Later information may be obtained from the appropriate County Council

The representation on this map of any other road, track or path is no evidence of the existence of a right of way.

WALKS AND TOURS (All Scales)

7 👣   Start point of walk

➡   Route of walk

Line of walk

Alternative route

3 🚗   Start point of tour

➡   Route of tour

Featured tour

Key to Atlas pages

Distances in miles to CIRENCESTER
Map Ref: 93 SP 0201

Birmingham	66	London	95
Bristol	39	Northampton	72
Cardiff	75	Oxford	35
Coventry	57	Reading	55
Hereford	49	Worcester	43

COTSWOLDS

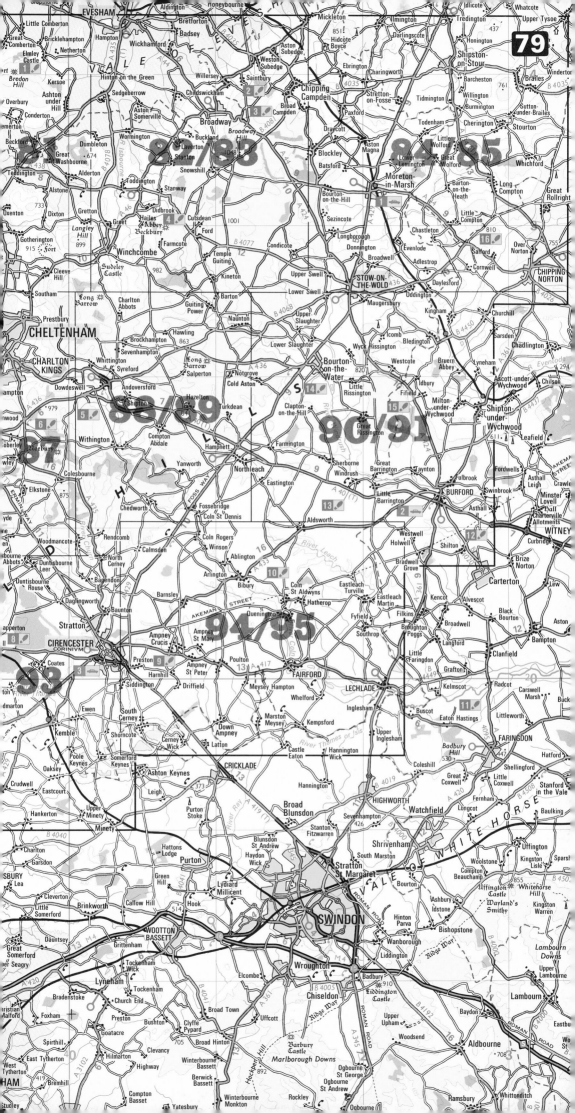

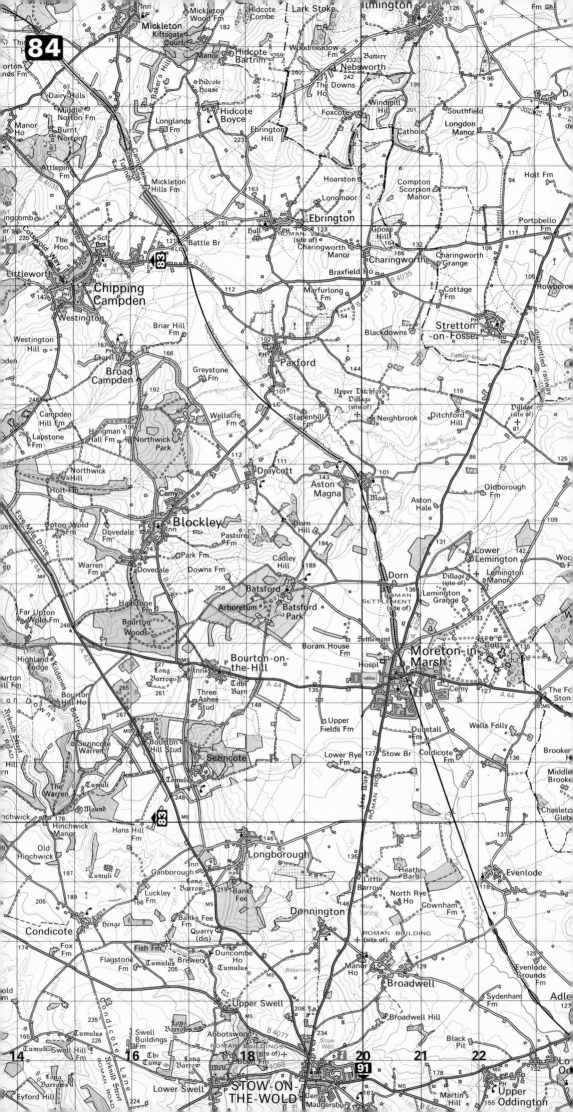

TOUR *1* 65 MILES
The North Wolds and Vale of Evesham

The steep escarpment of the Cotswolds with its stone-built houses contrasts with the timber and thatch of the lush, fruit-growing Vale of Evesham on this tour. The route veers north to give a taste of Shakespeare's country along the Avon, allows for detours to Hidcote Gardens and Broadway Tower Country Park, and returns via Chipping Campden.

The drive starts from Moreton-in-Marsh (see page 56), a small, busy town of the northern wolds on the Foss Way, which forms its wide main street. The bell in the 16th-century Curfew Tower was tolled daily until 1860.

Follow the Oxford road A44 for 1¾ miles. Here the road passes the Four Shire Stone where the counties of Gloucestershire, Oxfordshire and Warwickshire (and, before the last boundary changes, Worcestershire) meet. *After ¾ mile turn right onto an unclassified road for Chastleton. Half a mile on turn left and cross a cattle grid, then at the end turn right onto the A44. Beyond the Cross Hands public house turn left onto an unclassified road, signed Rollright.* Two miles ahead on the right, lie the Rollright Stones (see page 61), two curious Bronze Age clusters of stones situated on a high ridge with wide views.

Turn left ¾ mile past the Stones, signed Stratford, and descend, via Long Compton, to Shipston-on-Stour. Turn left onto the Campden road B4035, and after 1¾ miles cross the main road. In 1½ miles keep forward onto an unclassified road via Charingworth to the pretty village of Ebrington. At the end of the main street bear right and then right again, signed The Hidcotes, keep forward for 2 miles then turn right for Hidcote Manor Gardens (see page 54). Cultivated by an American and now owned by the National Trust, Hidcote is a series of small gardens, each given over to a theme or a kind of flower. Kiftsgate Court Garden with its special collection of roses is just opposite Hidcote on the unclassified road.

Return to the T-junction, turn left and then take the next turning on the right, signed Mickleton. At the main road turn right and immediately right again onto the A46, signed Stratford, to enter Mickleton. At the end of the village bear left, then in ½ mile go forward onto an unclassified road, signed Long Marston, and continue to Welford-on-Avon. After crossing the river, turn left onto the A439 to Bidford-on-Avon. Shakespeare is said to have been drunk at the Falcon Inn.

At the roundabout take the first exit onto the B4085, signed Broadway, and cross the 15th-century bridge. After ½ mile turn right for Cleeve Prior and South Littleton. One mile beyond South Littleton go over a level crossing, then take the first turning left onto an unclassified road (no sign) to reach Bretforton where the B4035 is joined, and continue to Weston Subedge.

At the Seagrave Arms turn right onto the A46, signed Cheltenham, pass through Willersley, and in 1¾ miles at the T-junction turn right onto the A44 into Broadway (see page 40). Both Charles I and Cromwell used the 17th-century Lygon Arms, and the Pre-Raphaelite artists spent time here at the end of the last century.

By the Swan Hotel turn left onto an unclassified road, signed Snowshill. Ascend and later bear right into the secluded village of Snowshill (see page 63). The Tudor manor houses a collection of clocks, toys and musical instruments and has a lovely terraced garden.

Turn left at the church, then at the top go forward over the crossroads, signed Chipping Campden and Broadway Tower (care required). After 1¼ miles turn left, signposted Broadway, to Broadway Tower (see page 40). At over 1,000 feet the views from the 18th-century tower are magnificent. Other attractions are an adventure playground and a collection of rare animals and birds.

Just past the Fish Hill Picnic Area cross the main road, signed Saintbury, and after ¾ mile turn right, signed Chipping Campden. Continue for 1½ miles and at the crossroads turn right for Chipping Campden (see page 43). A former centre of the wool industry, the town has an impressive 15th-century 'wool' church and a fine Jacobean Market Hall standing in the centre of the High Street. Craft work is kept alive at the pottery and the Campden Weavers.

Leave the town by Sheep Street B4081, signed Broad Campden, and after ¼ mile turn left onto an unclassified road for Broad Campden. In the village turn right then shortly right again and climb to Blockley (see page 37). Turn left then shortly right onto the B4479, signed Moreton-in-Marsh. After 1½ miles at the T-junction turn left onto the A44 to pass through Bourton-on-the-Hill (see page 38), before returning to Moreton-in-Marsh.

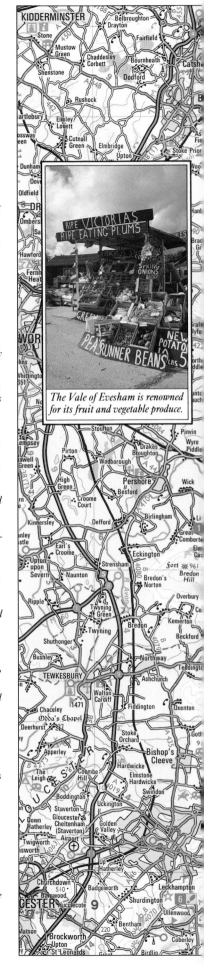

The Vale of Evesham is renowned for its fruit and vegetable produce.

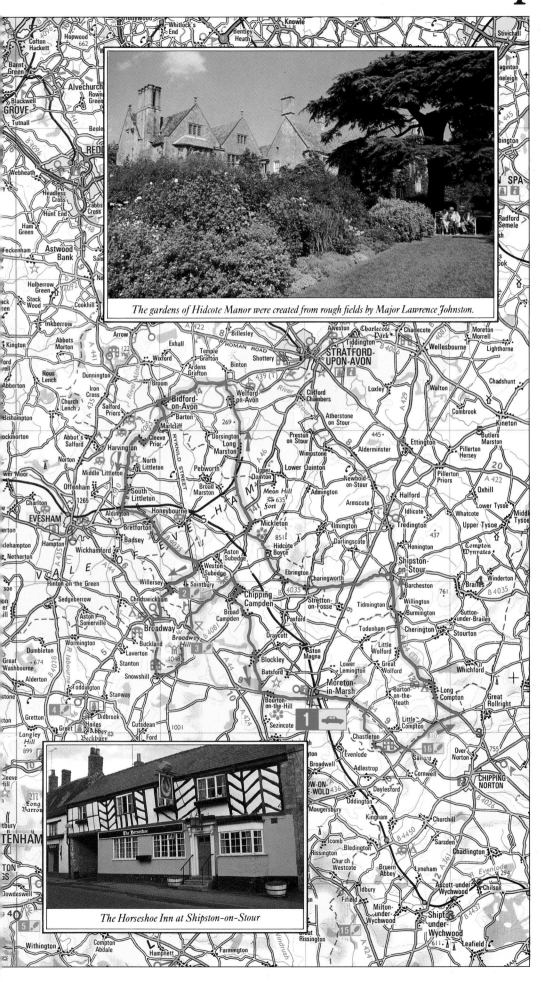

The gardens of Hidcote Manor were created from rough fields by Major Lawrence Johnston.

The Horseshoe Inn at Shipston-on-Stour

TOUR2 71 MILES
Central Cotswold Towns and Villages

From Oxfordshire to Gloucestershire this drive passes through several villages along the River Windrush, also taking in the hill towns of Chipping Norton and Stow-on-the-Wold. The ruins of 13th-century Hailes Abbey and the 15th-century manor at Minster Lovell indicate the splendours of a former age, and Birdland and Cotswold Farm Park are essential stopovers for the nature lover.

The drive starts at Burford (see page 41), formerly an important crossroads of the coaching era. *From the Corner House Hotel halfway down the High Street follow the Swinbrook road, unclassified, and after 1 mile turn left. After another mile continue straight over the crossroads, signed Asthall.* The drive then skirts Asthall, where there is a fine Elizabethan manor-house (not open).

At the T-junction turn right, signed Witney, and at the top of an ascent turn left onto the B4047. In 1¾ miles at Minster Lovell (see page 56) turn left onto the unclassified road, then bear right. In ¼ mile turn left over the river bridge. The ruins of its 15th-century manor-house can be seen to the right. *In 2 miles at the crossroads turn left to reach Leafield. Turn left, signed Shipton, then in 2 miles cross the main road and continue on into Shipton-under-Wychwood (see page 63).* Originally set in Wychwood Forest, this large Oxfordshire village boasts a 600-year-old hostelry formerly used as a guesthouse for Bruern Abbey.

Here the drive turns right onto the A361 and continues to Chipping Norton (see page 43). Follow the Stow road B4450 via Churchill and attractive Bledington, and later join the A436 for Stow-on-the-Wold (see page 65). A good antiques centre, this hill-top town also hosts two horse fairs annually.

From the town square turn right onto the A429, then turn left, signed Tewkesbury (B4077), and immediately branch left B4077 for Upper Swell. The B4077 continues through Ford, then after 1½ miles descends to the Stanway war memorial. Here turn right at the crossroads, signed Stanton, onto an unclassified road. Pass the Jacobean gatehouse and grounds of Stanway House (see page 65), and after 1¼ miles turn right for Stanton (see page 64). The architect, Sir Philip Stott, was lord of the manor here at the beginning of this century and restored many of the buildings.

Bear left, signed Broadway, then after ¾ mile turn left onto the A46 Cheltenham road. Go straight over the Toddington roundabout and after 1 mile take the second turning on the left onto an unclassified road for Hailes Abbey (see page 52). The 13th-century ruins are now National Trust property, and a small museum contains some interesting exhibits.

Return for 200 yards and turn left, then follow a narrow byroad to climb onto the Roel Hill ridge (nearly 1,000ft) from where there are fine views. At the T-junction turn left, then take the next turning right. At the next T-junction turn left and continue to Guiting Power (see page 52). After ½ mile at the T-junction turn right, signed Andoversford, then take the next turning on the left, signed Stow. After 1¾ miles a detour can be made by turning left at the crossroads to the Cotswold Farm Park, where rare breeds of livestock are on view.

The main drive keeps forwards and follows a quiet country road to Lower Swell. Here turn right onto the B4068, then left onto an unclassified road, signed The Slaughters (see page 63). The Elizabethan manor-house in Upper Slaughter is open on Friday afternoons during summer. *At the end of the village, turn left for the neighbouring village of Lower Slaughter.* Bridges cross the River Eye, which turns the waterwheel of the 19th-century corn mill.

Cross the road bridge, then turn right and at the end right again onto the A429, signed Cirencester. Turn left after ½ mile onto an unclassified road into Bourton-on-the-Water (see page 38). There is something of interest for everyone here: Birdland and the Butterfly Exhibition, a model railway exhibition and a motor museum, a perfumery and a scale model of the village at the Old New Inn.

At the post office turn right into the village centre, then at the crossroads turn left onto the unclassified Sherborne road. Cross the river and bear right, then ascend and, after 4 miles, turn left for Sherborne. At the end of the village turn right and continue to the village of Windrush. The church preserves a splendid Norman doorway and the churchyard is graced with some remarkable 18th-century table tombs. *Keep left and after ¾ mile turn left at the T-junction to Great Barrington (see page 35). At the war memorial bear right for Taynton. At the end of the village follow the signs for Burford, and, after 1 mile, join the A424. In ¼ mile at the mini-roundabout turn right onto the A361 and cross the river bridge for the return to Burford.*

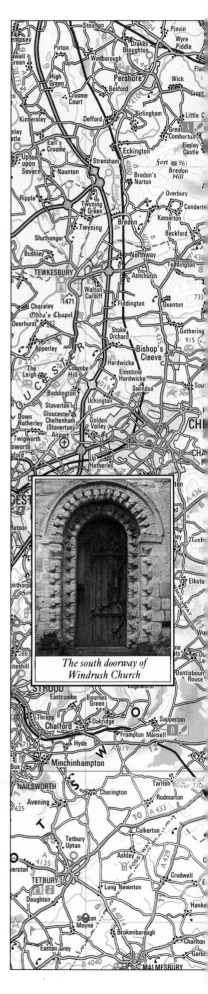

The south doorway of Windrush Church

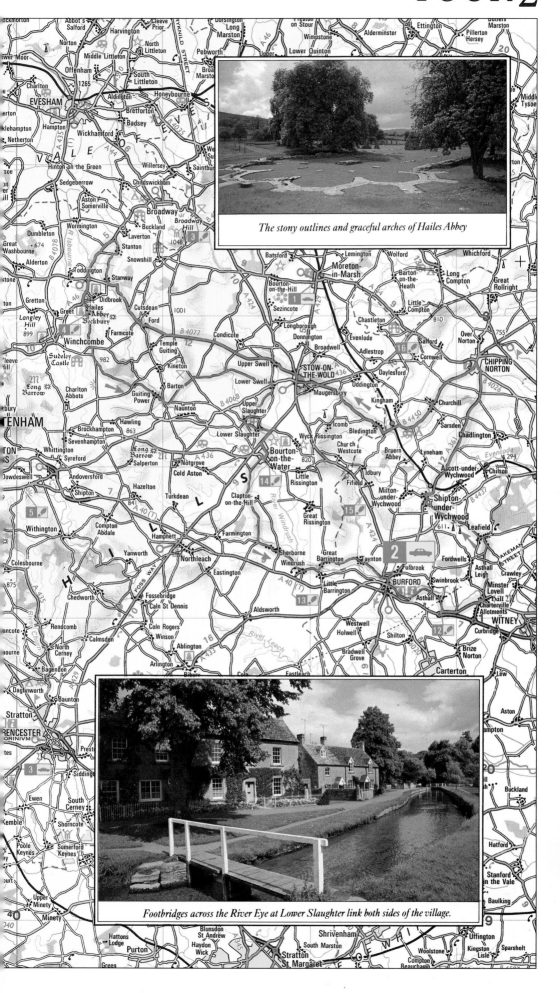

The stony outlines and graceful arches of Hailes Abbey

Footbridges across the River Eye at Lower Slaughter link both sides of the village.

TOUR3 67 MILES
The Infant Thames

From Cirencester, the Roman capital of the Cotswolds, the route
follows the Thames from its reputed source, through Ewen and Ashton
Keynes to its confluence with the Coln and the Leach at Lechlade.
Passing through some of the smaller villages of the Coln valley, it allows
for detours to the Cotswold Water Park and Wildlife Park.

The drive starts from Cirencester (see page 44), a pleasant market town
situated at the junction of three Roman roads. The Norman abbey gateway still
stands, and the 15th-century 'wool' church has a magnificent three-storeyed
porch, which was once used as the town hall. The 3,000 acres of Cirencester
Park nearby are open to the public.

*From Cirencester follow signs The South West and Chippenham to leave by the
A429. In 1½ miles go forward onto the A433, signed Bristol. After another mile, in
the meadows to the right, beyond the turning for Coates, is the reputed source
of the River Thames. Pass under a railway bridge and turn left onto an unclassified
road for Kemble. Cross the main road into the village, then go over the staggered
crossroads, signed Ewen.* The infant Thames is first seen before reaching Ewen.

*Continue with the South Cerney signs and keep forward at all crossroads. In South
Cerney (see page 64) turn right at the war memorial into Broadway Lane, and in ¾
mile pass, on the right, the Cotswold Marina.* This is part of the Cotswold Water
Park, a series of nearly 100 lakes offering a variety of water-based activities,
such as fishing, sailing, water-skiing, windsurfing and powerboat racing. *Half a
mile farther, at the crossroads, turn right, signed Ashton Keynes. In 1¼ miles turn left
and shortly branch left to reach Ashton Keynes.* The stripling Thames, only a few
feet wide, flows through the village and is spanned by small bridges.

*At the end of the village turn left onto the Cricklade road then bear right. Two miles
farther, at the crossroads, turn left onto the B4040, and after another 1½ miles turn
left again to enter Cricklade. At the clock tower turn right and follow signs Swindon,
then in ¾ mile join the A419. One mile farther turn left onto an unclassified road for
Castle Eaton. This pleasant Thames-side village is skirted by continuing with the
Highworth road to pass through Hannington. In 1¼ miles turn left onto the B4019
for Highworth.* A hill-top town with some 17th-century houses, Highworth has
a 15th-century church which still bears the marks of a Civil War cannon-ball.

*Turn left onto the Stow road, A361. After 4½ miles, on the left, a riverside park is
passed before crossing the old Halfpenny Bridge into Lechlade (see page 55).* Here,
where the rivers Coln and Leach join the Thames, one can enjoy boating and
fishing. *Turn right, then right again to leave by the Faringdon road A417, and in ¾
mile cross St John's Bridge.* Motor cruisers and narrow boats cannot navigate the
Thames beyond this point. Two miles farther the drive passes the grounds of
Buscot Park, an 18th-century house built in the Adam style and surrounded by
a landscaped garden. *Keep straight ahead to Faringdon.* This market town has a
Georgian market hall and several old inns. *From the Market Square branch left
onto the Bampton road A4095, and after passing the church turn left. In 2½ miles
cross Radcot Bridge.* Built early in the 14th century, this bridge is the oldest to
span the Thames.

*At Clanfield the drive goes forward onto the Burford road B4020 for Alvescot. In ¼
mile turn left (unclassified) to Kencot, and in 1¼ miles at the crossroads turn right into
Filkins (see page 50).* The Cotswold Woollen Weavers keep old skills alive in an
18th-century barn, and there is a small museum and an old village lock-up. *In
the village turn right and in 1 mile, at the T-junction, turn right onto the A361, signed
Stow. In 2 miles at the crossroads turn left (unclassified), signed Wildlife Park, and
pass the entrance to the Cotswold Wildlife Park.* Set in 200 acres of lake-watered,
wooded parkland, it contains animals and birds from all over the world. There
is also an adventure playground and a narrow-gauge railway.

*In ½ mile go over the crossroads, signed Eastleach Martin, then at the end of a
tree-lined road (½ mile) branch left and follow a narrow byroad to the twin
Eastleaches.* Linked by a road bridge and a stone footbridge, these two
unspoiled villages face each other across the River Leach. *At Eastleach Martin
cross the River Leach into Eastleach Turville, then keep right through the village on the
Hatherop road. In ½ mile at the T-junction turn left, then in ½ mile turn right, and
two miles farther turn right again into Hatherop. Turn left for Coln St Aldwyns (see
page 47).* There is a mainly Norman church with a fine tower, an Elizabethan
manor-house and some 17th-century cottages.

Turn left, signed Fairford, then cross the River Coln and ascend into Quenington.
The church here is notable for its two richly-carved Norman doorways.

*At the green turn left, then at the end of the village recross the Coln and continue to
Fairford (see page 50).* The magnificent stained-glass windows of the late
15th-century church depict the Biblical story from the Creation to the Last
Judgement. The River Coln provides good fishing waters, and there is an
interesting old mill. *The drive returns to Cirencester by following the A417 through
the pleasant villages of Poulton and Ampney Crucis (see page 34).*

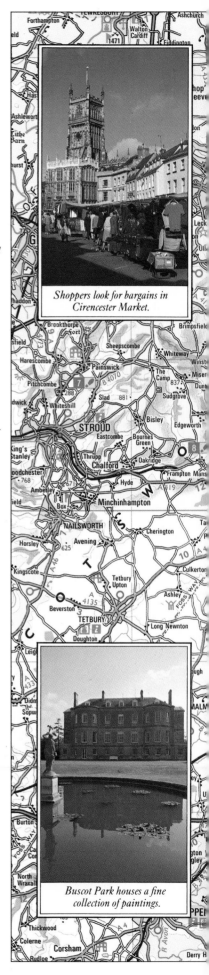

Shoppers look for bargains in
Cirencester Market.

Buscot Park houses a fine
collection of paintings.

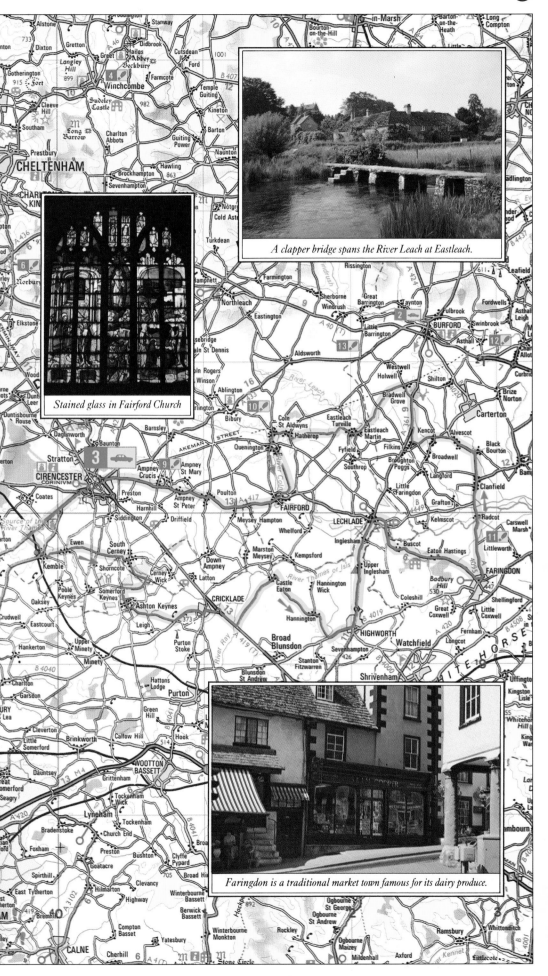

A clapper bridge spans the River Leach at Eastleach.

Stained glass in Fairford Church

Faringdon is a traditional market town famous for its dairy produce.

WALK 1
In Summertime on Bredon

Allow 2½ hours

I cannot think of a more satisfying experience than to lie atop Bredon's breezy scarp in summertime and while away some hours in blissful contemplation, to 'see the coloured counties and hear the larks so high' to quote from a poem by A E Housman, published in *A Shropshire Lad*. There is a steep climb initially up to Bredon Hill but it is well worth it for the panoramic views.

Park either along the wide-verged Kersoe road or in the broad main street of Elmley Castle (GR982412). Elmley Castle is in many ways the archetypal English village. Its qualities can be admired in a wider context during this walk. The route rises in triumphant fashion to Bredon's crest before returning to the vale close by the massive bracken-covered earthworks of 12th-century Beauchamp Castle. *Take the road leading north-west from the Queen Elizabeth, passing the former post office (closed 1984) and several delightful half-timbered cottages, and bear left with the lane to Hill House Farm. A bridleway leads on up a hollow way to a gate. Stay on the main track climbing between Doctor's Wood and Fox Hill Wood to a stile/gate at the edge of Even Hill. At this point, where the track peters out, turn sharp left along the top side of Doctor's Wood. Join the green track which rises out of the wood, gaining height steadily, until, at a gate into Long Plantation, turn right up the worn path by the short edge of woodland. Keep right,*

away from the wood above the scrub line, on course for the scarp edge.

Follow the scarp-top track via two gates to accompany the wall to Parson's Folly. Erected by the owner of Woollas Hall as a prospect tower, the viewing platform sets the spectator at 1,000ft. Unfortunately the tower is now used for some serious purpose and it hums with electrical apparatus. The Banbury Stone was believed to have been used ceremonially during the Iron Age occupation of the double-ramparted hill-fort.

On a clear day few visitors will not be impressed by the view of a fertile vale dotted with towns and villages, woodland and orchard, a densely cropped patchwork. The hillscape is rewarding too: to the east, Edge Hill with the long line of the Cotswold escarpment running south to Stinchcombe Hill; further south-west and across the Severn, the Forest of Dean, May Hill and the Monnow Hills; the Malvern range and, beyond them, the Black Mountains to the west; Brown Clee and Abdon Burf to the north-west with Abberley Hill in front and The Wrekin in the far distance beyond; and, due north, the Clent and Lickey Hills, just south of Birmingham.

Retrace your steps, keeping to the wire fence and skirting the top of Long Plantation, until the Wychavon Way waymarks (yellow crown) direct you left down through the scarp woodland and rough pastures by two hunting gates. Pass en route a moated site of medieval origin and today a home only for ducks, before eventually reaching the Kersoe road where you go left. Take the opportunity of inspecting the parish church before you leave for it contains a model and detailed history of Beauchamp Castle and dynasty together with several interesting memorials, notably that of the Earls of Coventry from Croome Court near Pershore, who were responsible for building Broadway Tower (WALK 3).

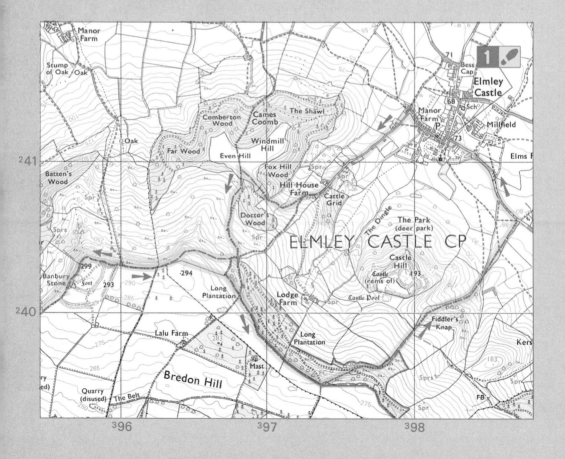

Olympick Edge

Allow 1 hour

A short walk, embracing the Dover's Hill scarp, that can conveniently be extended to include Chipping Campden, an elegant Cotswold medieval wool centre with the

appropriate motto 'History in Stone'. The golds and rusts of autumn will enhance the views, but the long grass on the hill may be wet and the wood muddy, so stout shoes or wellingtons would be advisable.

From the Dover's Hill National Trust car park (GR136395) go through the kissing gate and follow the escarpment edge straight ahead. The expansive northward views feature Dumbleton and Bredon Hills backed by the Malvern range; below spreads the Vale of Evesham, green and fertile, dotted with greenhouses. Evesham (to the north-west) is backed by the wooded Lench Hills and, as far as the eye can see, the undulating countryside of Worcestershire and Warwickshire.

At Bold Gap the path descends slightly towards a wooded squeeze stile. Do not cross this stile; instead, descend the pasture, passing a waymark post, to reach a stile into Lynches Wood. The term 'lynches' suggests a terraced hillside, a not uncommon scarp feature, though the walk fails to reveal any evidence of these ancient cultivation strips. It is thought that these strip lynchets were often used during the Romano-British period for vineyards. Indeed, directly below the woodland fruit orchards still exist.

The OS map shows none of the paths within this wooded spur, so heed the yellow-painted waymarks guiding along the main path round the spur. *Cross a heavily used path, and where the path forks go left, then after a short descent turn sharp left at the path junction. The route rises gradually, beneath sweet chestnuts and laurel bushes, until it turns left up recently set steps. Swing right at the top, following a*

fence-line and still within the wood, to a stile. Go over the stile and take an old cart track, just discernible ahead and right, following the fence up the pasture near the woodland. Notice the old ridge and furrow on the shallow slope just above Lynches Wood.

The track mounts the rough slope characterised by hummocks symptomatic of the unstable nature of the underlying clays, which slip and thus intensify the scarp effect. It then slants right about the woodland, rising above a scrub-surrounded spring pool. Just before the road divert left along a waymarked hollow way to the elegant topograph. Suggestive of a garden sundial stand, the topograph was erected to mark the considerable efforts, notably of F L Griggs, to acquire this estate for the healthy recreation of the public when, in the mid-1920s, exclusive hotel development threatened to deny access. Notice boards in the car park outline the details of the history of the Dover's Hill Olympick Games and the National Trust property in general.

A fine way of developing a walk from this location is by following the Cotswold Way waymarks to Kingcomb Lane, then down Hoo Lane to explore Chipping Campden. Stroll along the curving High Street to the impressive Perpendicular 'wool' church at Berrington, returning by Sheep Street, Westington and Blind Lane into Dyer's Lane for Dover's Hill.

WALK 3
Towering over Broadway

Allow 2½ hours

Because Pershore Abbey held the Broadway estate prior to the Dissolution of the Monasteries by Henry VIII, the hill pastures immediately surrounding the village of Broadway are in Worcestershire. This escarpment walk embraces probably the most popular village of this predominantly vale shire. The climb up to Broadway Tower is strenuous, however.

From the Fish Hill picnic site (GR120369) follow the 'Woodland Walk' footpath sign, past the Don Russell memorial topograph, and into the quarries along a clearly waymarked path. Continue high through Campden Hole beech woods, following the signs for Broadway. In due course the path descends to a stile and crosses the minor road by the entrance to Farncombe House (Group 4 Security headquarters). Cross the stile, descend the pasture, slanting gently down from the fence to a stile vividly painted red and white! Occasional waymark posts plot the line of the footpath via a gateway and stile down to Pike Cottage (the site of the turnpike gate) in Broadway's main street.

The houses in upper Broadway are 'very grand'. Top and Orchard Farms are far removed from simple agricultural dwellings. All the buildings in this part of the village suffer from clamorous traffic throttling up in preparation for the ascent of Fish Hill. Although the walk does not go through Broadway take the opportunity of strolling down the 'broad way' noticing the Lygon Arms and the pleasing and harmonious mixture of Cotswold cottage and house styles. The original 'broad way'

is probably the present Snowshill Road where both Broadway Court and the old parish church, St Eadburgh's, are situated. This church dedication derives from a patron saint of Pershore Abbey, the abbots of which had their summer grange here. Evidence of this can be found along the new 'broad way' in the Prior's Manse, by the junction of Leamington Road and Abbot's Grange situated just below The Green; both are dated circa 1320.

The next stage of the walk climbs to Broadway Tower, dominating the scarp at 1,027ft, making it a superb objective. *Branch from the main street at Peartree House, a Cotswold Way footpath sign directs along a lane and over two stiles/gates into a small pasture. The well-trod footpath is easy to follow as it slants left via stiles and up old ridge and furrow. Steadily gain height, keeping alongside a wall through arable fields to enter the Broadway Tower Country Park through the hunting gate.* If you wish to climb the prospect tower or explore the country park, tickets can be purchased during opening hours 10 a.m.–6 p.m. Built on a beacon site in 1798 at the whim of the Countess of Coventry (wife of the sixth Earl), Broadway Tower commands a memorable view across the Midland Counties. The Earl owned the nearby Spring Hill estate in which the tower was at that time situated.

Depart through the hunting gate to the east of the tower slipping through the scrubby lateral valley, a slip trough created by the downward movement of fractured limestone bedrock on the unstable clay bed. Follow the route to a stile/gate to the Armley Bank woodland. Armley is an interesting placename deriving from the Saxon for 'wretched', the inference being 'wood of the beggars or outlaws'.

Proceed along the Cotswold Way to cross Fish Hill road by the Fish Inn. The inn was originally a summer-house for Farncombe House before becoming an ale house to provide refreshments for weary, thirsty travellers at the crest of the steep pull up Broadway Hill. *Cross the road (with great care because it is usually very busy) to the Fish Hill Picnic Site, thus completing the outing.*

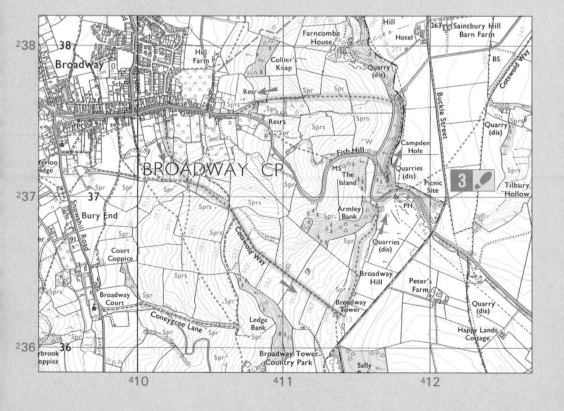

defences on two sides.

The route follows the Cotswold Way keeping to the scarp bounding wall. Just short of the old wooded quarry go through a gate, left, keeping to the stone wall. On joining the trackway, turn right through the gate. Along Campden Lane sheep were driven and wagons drawn, relaying the fleeces of the 'Cotswold Lion' to Chipping Campden to be stapled (graded) by the medieval merchants before despatch to London and Southampton for export to France and Italy.

The main track branches left, but go through a gate onto the bridleway, where it can get muddy in places. Beyond a small and revealing freestone quarry you

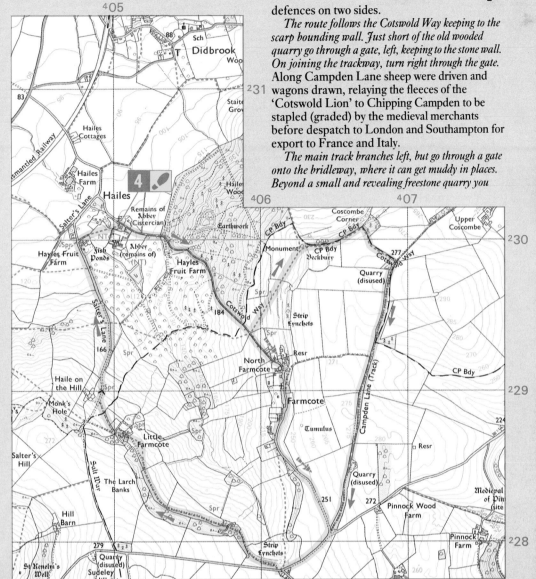

Sheep, Salt and Saints

Allow 2¼ hours

Beginning at Hailes Abbey, a place of pilgrimage for three centuries, this walk takes in part of the Cotswold Way, an ancient drove route to Chipping Campden and a former salt way to Lechlade.

Start from the Hailes Abbey car park (GR051301). Follow the road east and at the Hayles Fruit Farm continue up the waymarked roughly cobbled track. The lane leads up between Hailes Wood and fruit orchards to a stile and signpost to Beckbury Camp, left. You may prefer to shorten the walk to Lynes Barn by following the lane through the medieval grange of Great Farmcote to visit the Norman chapel at ease.

The main route ascends the pasture from the lane. Cross to a gate at the end of a fence, then via a stile head up into Cromwell's Clump, the monument at the north-west corner of Beckbury hill-fort. The four-acre hill-fort is protected by natural scarp

reach the Farmcote road and bear left towards Winchombe. Continue downhill to Lynes Barn, and, a few yards beyond the road junction, go through the gate right. Follow the waymarked track along a strip lynchet shelf (terraced hillside), past a Dutch barn to a double gate. The route proceeds by gates through a short section of woodland, following the contours to Little Farmcote Farm. Through the iron gate keep right, round the new barn, before rising through the farmyard and right onto the concrete road. Turn right on the tarmacked Salter's Lane, descending over a cattle grid. Salt was carried from Droitwich to Lechlade and on to London via the Thames. *Turn right just beyond the few houses on the right along a short lane, following the Cotswold Way, and from the gate cross the pasture diagonally to another gate.* After the rigours of the walk enjoy the relaxing atmosphere of Hailes Abbey and St Nicholas' Church with its superb medieval wall paintings.

A churchyard lych gate

*Farm scene
in the
19th century*

O'er Hill and Dell

Allow 1¾ hours

The Kilkenny Viewpoint car park on Cold Comfort Common (GR004186) overlooking the Chelt Valley provides an excellent springboard for a high wold walk, returning by delving into the remote wooded Hilcot Valley.

Commence on the Hilcot road passing the mast and St Paul's Epistle, a larch clump set upon a mound at 948ft. This curious placename emanates from the practice of reading biblical passages whilst beating the bounds of the Dowdeswell parish. That it occurs on the summit of a hill is unusual but quite understandable, symbolising St Paul's message of faith being 'spread over all the world'. The panorama stretches north to the Malvern Hills and south to the distant Thamesdown Hills above Swindon.

Branch from the road just prior to entering a belt of beeches, go left to a stile, then, keeping strictly to the footpath, go through the tiny reservoir enclosure via stiles. The route accompanies the ridge wall with fine views over Foxcote and the upper Coln valley, with the richly textured woodland of Foxcote Grove a pleasing feature on the nearer slope. *Join a track leading on over Withington Hill, alongside a fence to a gate, go immediately right through the gate (modifying the true course of the bridleway), and follow the track leading down beside Smoke Acre.* The name derives from land held by the payment of a money-tax (known as 'smoke pennies') in place of tithewood. *The track passes through a new gate beneath the word 'Acre' on the map, continuing under powerlines, whose imposing pylons and wires do nothing to enhance this (or any) view.*

Leave the track at a metal gate left, shortly before the track veers right following the field boundary. The path goes right, along the top of the bank, through the scrub, which appears more impenetrable than it actually is. Entering a narrow cultivated strip, the path slants down the steep bank left, where the bracken ceases, to reach a hunting gate at the foot of a dry valley. A lane

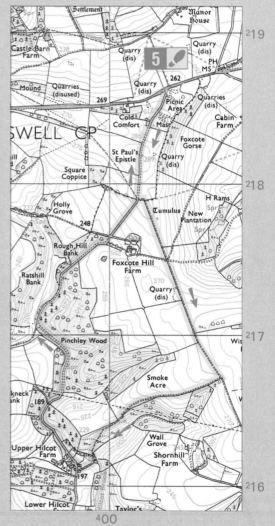

crosses the Hilcot Brook with its pretty pond, and rises via a gate to the road. Go right past the attractive buildings of Upper Hilcot Farm.

The walk follows the minor road for Cold Common, initially beside the crystal waters of Hilcot Brook, constantly sheltered by wooded banks. These wooded hillsides are alive with the song of birds, indeed, the name Pinchley meant 'the clearing frequented by finches'. Breakneck Bank refers to the steepness of the slope and Ratshill was 'rat infested', though you are more likely to encounter tree-rats (squirrels)!

The road, a glorified woodland way, rises by Rough Hill Bank to regain the open road on Cold Common.

Devil's Chimney

Allow 3 hours

An invigorating and easily followed walk on firm ground with superb scarp and wold views, intriguing quarries and a pretty village with notable connections.

Park at the Seven Springs layby (GR966169). The springs form the highest water rising of the River Thames via the River Churn, its longest tributary, although inexplicably Thames Head south-west of Cirencester is deemed the source. *Walk north-east to the staggered crossroads of the A436 with the A435, turn left and left again along the minor road.* The route to Ullenwood Manor coincides with the Cotswold Way and, as such, is extremely well waymarked, distinguished by a white spot above waymark arrows.

The walk branches left rising with the hedge then a wall, as it skirts the escarpment through briars and brambles onto Charlton King's Common revealing breathtaking views over Cheltenham and the Severn Vale. There are numerous hollows in the gorse due to the extraction of shellag ragstones for drystone walling. *The route crosses the hill-fort to a*

sign directing right for the Devil's Chimney. This appears to have been created around 1780 by quarrymen, partly because the stone was inferior to requirements and partly as a jolly gimmick. Over recent years erosion has threatened its very existence, but in 1985 remedial action was undertaken to support the frail fractured pinnacle with iron rods and mortar, so Cheltonians will for a few more years have their romantic myth.

Return to the path along the edge south, passing old quarry incursions and Salterley Grange Quarry. Descend to the road then turn left uphill till a signpost to Ullenwood directs right down a bridle track. At the Ullenwood road go left past the Cotswold Hill Golf Clubhouse; cross the A436 onto the Cowley road, and branch immediately right at the double gates onto the unenclosed track rising onto South Hill.

At the top of the hill turn left along the track passing Cuckoopen Barn. Notice the silver plaque by the gate proclaiming 'the World's Biggest Straw Rick' – 40,400 bales, achieved in 1982. The farmhouse and barns have been erected since. *The bridle track descends the ridge via gates passing an unusually lowly set long barrow above Coldwell Bottom. Upon reaching the road go forward, taking the left turn off the road, beside the wall (not down the inviting hollow way) passing Close Farm. Continue down the pasture to a stile and footbridge rising to a kissing gate.* Walkers are encouraged to take the spur route right, down the road to visit St Giles church.

Return to the village, transferred, as the map shows, from a site east of the church, and follow the street up past the school onto a trackway, branching right along a narrowly fenced footpath back to Seven Springs.

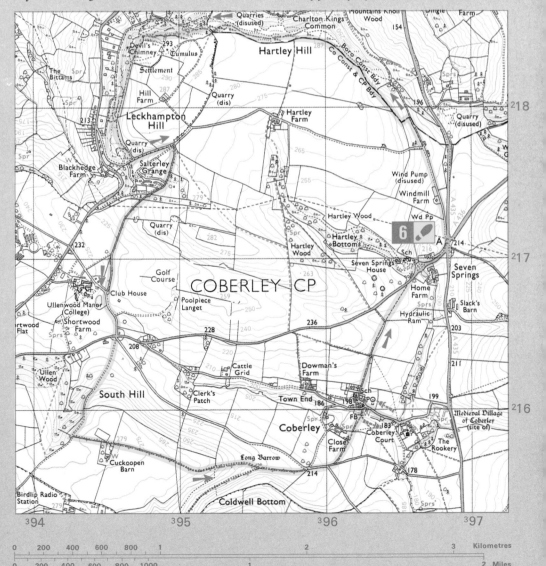

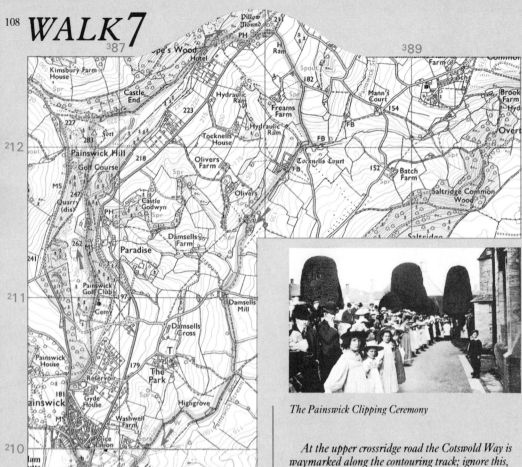

The Painswick Clipping Ceremony

Prospect over Paradise

Allow 2¼ hours

This walk enjoys the liberty and spacious views of Painswick Beacon looking across the Severn Vale to the Forest of Dean and the nearby wooded scarplands. It then returns in the intimacy of the Painswick Stream valley, passing Tocknell's Court and concluding via Painswick's famous churchyard.

Park in the free car park off Stamages Lane (GR865095). Walk up to the lych-gate and along New Street. This was new in medieval terms around 1260 and here several fine classical-styled houses face onto the churchyard. *At the crossroads, with the original main street coming up Bisley Street, turn left up Gloucester Street. Go out of the village beyond the Gyde Almshouses to a minor road right leading onto the Common. Branch left opposite the reservoir gates with the Cotswold Way, but do not follow the obvious track beside the plantation; go across the lower golf course fairway and an unenclosed road. Keep above the cemetery; soon to enter a woodland path, passing Catsbrain Quarry.* This curious name derives from 'cattes-brazen', a term applied to a mottling of rough clay mixed with stones.

At the upper crossridge road the Cotswold Way is waymarked along the contouring track; ignore this, however, and climb directly onto the high ramparts of Painswick Beacon and take in the view at 931ft. During the Civil War campaign Charles I is reputed to have likened the setting of the tiny community to the south of Kimsbury to 'paradise'. Certainly his troops would have thought so, encamped in the open within the hill-fort. The name Paradise stuck, and few even today would dispute the sentiment.

Descend north-east onto a track above Pope's Wood. Join the metalled lane leading down to the Royal William pub, turn left to the bus stop, then cross the A46 to descend a bridle track onto the minor road. Continue downhill, forking right (signposted Sheepscombe) to reach the valley bottom. Follow the private drive signposted Tocknell's Court beside the Painswick Stream. The 17th-century house, its gardens and outbuildings are beautifully kept. *Climb the stile between the stream and cattle grid, proceeding down the valley pasture upon a green way to a gate. The route is well waymarked with yellow arrows right, past the cottage, then slant left to the site of Oliver's Mill, ford the stream and advance via a series of stiles down the pastures to Damsells Mill. Cross the road to a plank then cross a stone slab stile. Continue above the deeply cut stream beside a fence, via two more stiles, then turn right to a gate.*

Three paths diverge at this point, one obviously up the fenced hollow way. Do not follow this, instead, follow the hedgeline left going through a gate. Pass an odd round house ruin, presumably associated with the old canal-like mill pond, to reach Highgrove. Cross the stile tight by the garage wall and follow the metalled road. At Verlands House turn right up into Painswick.

Notice Painswick Institute, home of the Gloucestershire Guild of Craftsmen's annual exhibition each August. In the churchyard yew trees line the pathways between the impressive 17th- and 18th-century Renaissance-styled table tombs, giving a roll call of the wealthy clothiers and merchants of the district.

Cotswold Craftsmen

Allow 1¾ hours

Sapperton and the Daneway represent an important focus of Cotswold industrial ambition, with their late 18th-century canal tunnelling and early 20th-century Arts and Crafts revivalism, practised to exquisite standards by Gimson and the Barnsley brothers. The walk takes a dive into the deeply incised and wooded Frome valley, and there are some steep and muddy places so it is advisable to wear stout boots or wellingtons.

Farmer resting on a stile

Continue until you descend to the Dane Lane minor road just above Daneway House. Dating from around 1250 this fine house was the home of the Hancox family continuously from 1397 to 1860, then at the beginning of the present century it

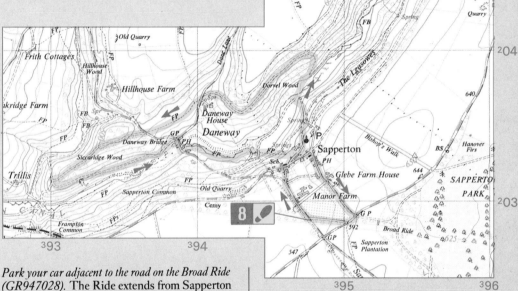

Park your car adjacent to the road on the Broad Ride (GR947028). The Ride extends from Sapperton Common east through Lord Bathurst's 10,000-acre Cirencester Park – only this length west of Sapperton Park is freely open to the public. *Go past the Manor Farm and the Glebe estate, then descend the footpath, right, into Sapperton village street, opposite the school and post office (there is no shop). Go right, then fork left down the 'no through road' to the parish church of St Kenelm.* The church belongs principally to the 14th-century, although the Atkyns family of Pinbury Park made embellishments around 1730. Sir Robert Atkyns, whose monument adorns the south transept, was the author of *The Ancient and Present State of Gloucestershire*, a famous early historical treatise. Pinbury was also the home of John Masefield, Poet Laureate.

Continue down the passage beside the church to a stile slanting below Upper Dorvel. This house was formed and extended from two cottages by Ernest Barnsley around 1901 and has a striking topiary. *Go over the stile and down, bearing right toward the sheep pens, keeping above them, then going through the third pen onto the steep road. Go left down a footpath,* which is prone to run as a water course after heavy rain. The footpath enters Dorvel Wood and becomes muddy. *Take the main, steep path upward and turn left along a main cross track,* which is also muddy in places, the result of the illicit passage of horses on the footpath.

became the workshop and showroom of the Gimson/Barnsley woodcraft partnership.

Cross the road to a stile and, keeping to the left track, proceed across Daneway Banks, a precious unimproved calcareous grassland, protected as a National Nature Reserve. Traverse to a gate then cross a minor road onto the obvious track through Siccaridge Wood, scrub woodland alive with wildlife. After a while descend to where three paths diverge, take sharp left down, eventually climbing a locked gate and crossing a pasture to reach Dane Lane next to the Daneway Inn. The pub was built for the refreshment of the bargees and professional 'leggers' who worked the Sapperton Canal Tunnel the two miles to Coates. The Thames and Severn Canal operated from 1789 to 1911, eventually being pensioned off by the Great Western Railway.

Take the footpath in the valley left by the bridge, signposted to Sapperton. Cross the stile stating 'Canal Walk'. Climb above the tunnel entrance to a stile, slanting up the pasture and keeping right of the old pump house, to a stile rising into Sapperton. Keep on the main road, past the village hall, Bell Inn and Glebe Farm, and continue to the road junction, where you go right. Notice the tiny railed enclosure left containing the precise Ordnance Survey datum 594.88ft. *Then go right again into the Broad Ride to conclude the walk.*

0	200	400	600	800		1			2			3	Kilometres

0	200	400	600	800	1000		1			2 Miles

SCALE 1:25000

WALK 9
Ampney Amble

Allow 2½ hours

A gentle stroll by leafy lanes visiting a church in a field and one in a beautiful village setting.

The A417 from Cirencester to Fairford has been re-aligned beyond The Crown pub and Harnhill Mill, making an excellent refuge to start this walk (GR073018). From the west access cross the main road and climb over the wooden field fence opposite (no stile or sign). Slant left across the arable field and follow the stream to a footbridge over an ancient ford. A stile and a wicket gate give access to St Mary's churchyard. Until the 1913 restoration it was known as 'the Ivy Church' as it had been neglected for many years. Originally the village of Ampney St Mary clustered round the church but it is presumed the community suffered when the Black Death struck in about 1349, and the village found a new footing upon Ash Brook ¾ mile distant. Enter St Mary's Church through a massive 14th-century elm door to view its splendid medieval wall paintings. Outside, above the blocked north door, is a tympanum of a lion trampling upon a two-headed serpent, a motif unique in England.

Cross the A417 once more and go right along the pedestrian walk to Ampney St Peter, turning left up the attractive village street. Notice the unusual vernacular feature of double string courses on the second house on the right, also the sundial on the right wall of the house on the fork of the road. *Take the right fork.* St Peter's Church has a pleasing west tower at the end of an 11th-century nave; the

A kissing gate allows only one person to pass through at a time.

14th-century churchyard cross with neatly restored gable head is contemporary with that at nearby Ampney Crucis.

Continue along the lane, beyond the Rectory, turning right into the tree-shaded lane behind Eastington House. Enjoy the views of Ashbrook on the way to the Red Lion (public house) junction. Go left down the minor road, and at the Ampney St Mary signpost turn right along the lane to Poulton. Turn right into the village, passing Prescott's shop and the Falcon Inn. The name Poulton means 'farmstead by a pool'; though now in Gloucestershire, it was formerly a detached parish of Wiltshire. The late 17th-century manor-house is the principal building on view, while ¾ mile south-west stands Poulton Priory, built in 1895 upon the site of a Gilbertine priory.

Follow the A417 on the pedestrian walk until the 'Hartley Ayrshires' farm sign. Enter the farmyard here (permissible right of way), pass the farmhouse and continue along the lane to its junction with Charlham Lane. Go right, soon to accompany Ampney Brook past The Moor, a precious remnant of common land, to reach the A417 again. Conclude by crossing the road and returning left, along the pedestrian walk.

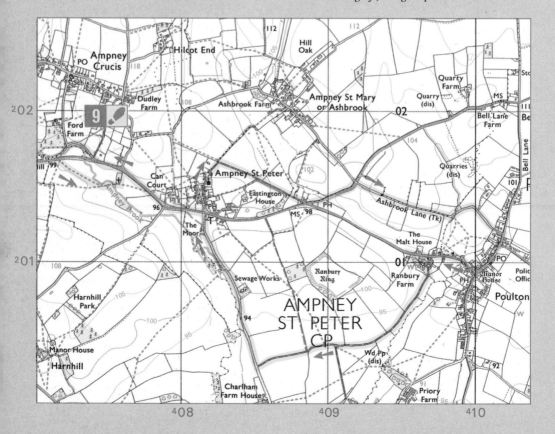

Beage's Stronghold

Allow 2¾ hours

The environs of the Coln are truly beautiful, clear waters running through river meadows sheltered by woodland and backed by sheep pastures and ubiquitous cornfields. But of all its splendours none surpasses the romantic charm of Bibury, 'discovered' by William Morris and adored by all who have passed this way ever since.

The minor road between Bibury and Coln St Aldwyn offers good car parking (GR130064). Go east enjoying the spacious prospect across the wold landscape, especially into the Coln valley to the south. Beyond Keble Barn notice the track joining the road from the left; this is the Salt Way, used in medieval times by pack ponies conveying this essential commodity from Droitwich to Lechlade, and on by boat down the Thames to London. *Approaching Coln St Aldwyn from the final bend to the road junction, the road also coincides with Akeman Street. Turn right to reach the Green crossroads, facing which are two shops.* A visit to the parish church, signposted to the right, is recommended. Nestling to the rear of the 16th-century manor-house and having at least a 700-year history, the church is cruciform in plan with a Norman and Early English tower, dated around 1284.

Proceeding down the village street, pass the New Inn and old mill. Follow the causeway road and cross over the river bridge. At Yew Tree Lodge turn right and pass through two gates to a footpath sign. Advance along the river meadows to a gate with a bold Williamstrip signboard into mature woodland. Emerging shortly at a further gate, the obvious track leads to the rushy Coln banks, crossing once again the line of Akeman Street.

Fly fishermen jealously guard their river sport, and walkers are advised to avoid the water's edge for fear of disturbing the trout or sensitive anglers.

The footpath negotiates three gates to reach Shagborough Bottom and then crosses a stone stile, ascending the steep bank beside woodland to a wicket gate with a Bibury Court Estate notice. Keep to the clear track above Oxhill Wood. Take the obvious right turn via double gates down the lane towards Bibury Mill. Walk on beyond the gate by the sheep pen to a footpath sign which directs left up to a gate. Pass to the right of the cricket ground, admiring the delightful views through the trees onto Bibury. Slant right to either the kissing gate or, lower down, a stone stile, from where a path leads right, down to the rear of Arlington Row. Totally renovated in the late 1970s by Alfred Groves, these former weavers' cottages are now owned by the National Trust and make an attractive village scene. *Go left in front of the cottages and along the footpath beside the mill stream and Rack Island.* Upon reaching the main road take the time to visit either the trout hatchery or Arlington Mill Cotswold Country Museum. The latter is a stimulating folk collection assembled by the late and greatly respected David Verey.

Go right crossing the smart footbridge by the Swan Hotel. Turn right along the pedestrian walk beside the Coln. Continue into the quieter section of the village to visit the parish church. This has been a religious sanctuary since Saxon times. In the 8th century Bishop Wilfrith of Worcester made a grant of land by the Coln to Earl Leppa for the term of his life and that of his daughter Beage (indeed Bibury means 'Beage's stronghold'). *Go back up to the main road, turn right past the entrance to Bibury Court Hotel, and follow the road right beyond the mill lane, back to the starting point.* The giant loop of the Coln seen on the way to Grove Barn makes a superb finale.

WALK 11
William
Morris Country

Allow 3 hours

Radcot, which means 'the cottage thatched with reeds', has been the scene of many battles over the centuries. Even Cromwell recognised its importance when in 1645 he overcame the Royalist outpost of Faringdon House. During the 17th and 18th centuries wharves by the Swan Inn were used during the transportation of the famous freestone from the Burford locality on course to adorn the interiors of important buildings in Oxford and London. Today it is the scene of much pleasure-boat activity and, despite its remote setting, is a place well worth visiting.

Park in the riverside meadow (GR286995) to the north-east of 14th-century Radcot Bridge (small parking fee). This is the oldest recorded bridging point on the upper Thames, the earliest reference dating from AD 958. The present bridge with its two pointed arches was built in 1317 by the monks of Beaulieu Abbey. The central arch is a restoration from the time when Richard II and Henry Bolinbroke engaged in battle here in 1387. The smaller navigation bridge and the numerous locks were constructed in 1787 by the Thames and Severn Canal Company.

There are two ways of enjoying this stroll along the Thames: either take a summer cruise upstream to Buscot Lock before disembarking and walking downstream, or totally commit yourself to 'shanks's pony', the former being little faster than the latter.

Pass through the wicket gate on the north side of the navigation bridge proceeding, in close company with the river, by stiles and gates and passing several war-time pill boxes and Grafton Lock. Fishermen ensconce themselves in hollows along the bank and share

the river with pleasure boats and wildfowl. In high summer nettles are a potential hazard only on the corner prior to the lock.

After 2½ meandering miles join a track leading from the river into Kelmscot. Beyond an old stone barn a high wall shields one of the Cotswold's famous houses, Kelmscot Manor. From 1871–96 this was the country home of William Morris, the pre-Raphaelite socialist advocate. He lies buried in the churchyard. The Manor was restored by the Society of Antiquarians and is open to the public occasionally. To judge by the quality of the village farmhouses the locality knew prosperity around 1700, a time when traditional gables and mullioned windows were losing favour to the classical square box architectural form. The village flourished from both the river traffic and agriculture, its isolated situation in flat open country ensuring the air of rural continuity. Larks and doves circle and sing in timeless fashion here.

Take the lane to the right of the Plough Inn (a useful stopping point halfway through this walk), and where this enters an arable field go left along the hedge-line to a footbridge on course for the wooden Thames footbridge. You may prefer at this point to return along the Thames bank or to cross the Thames to enter the scattered parish of Eaton Hastings.

Diverge from the track left to a stile, follow the dyke beside arable fields and then a pasture, crossing three stiles (one a covered barbed wire affair), and rise across a track to a beautifully remote cottage. Cross the rails, turning immediately right to a stile. Head east across arable land to a stile and a footbridge, rather overgrown, over a brook north of The Grange. Continue to pass in front of Rhodes Farm, reaching a gate onto the minor road to Eaton Hastings church. Unlike Kelmscot, Eaton Hastings seems to have suffered cruelly in the 14th century from the Black Death, which virtually destroyed the community, clustered since at least the 11th century around the church. Eaton meant 'river farmstead', and today all that remains are amalgamated farms cropping vast acreages of wheat.

Go south along the road, branching left onto the Lower House Farm access road. Continue east via gates by Camden Farm, slant left to a stile beyond the wind pump, two further stiles lead to a long pasture, and thence follow the fence to a stile by Radcot Bridge.

SCALE 1:28400

Meadow Way

Allow 2½ hours

A sumptuous stroll visiting two gorgeous Windrush villages together with a 'lost' village and mansion.

Park at the Windrush Valley Park, Asthall Barrow (GR290102). Go left, descending the minor road to Asthall, and fork right to enter the village. The fork crosses the course of the Roman road, Akeman Street, which is a corrupt form of Aquamania, the Saxon folk name for Bath. *Go right at the Maytime Inn, formerly the Three Horse Shoes.* Here Bob Arnold, known to millions as Tom Forrest of *The Archers*, spent his youth when his father was publican. *Cross Asthall Bridge to a stile left into the meadow.* The River Windrush would appear to be living up to its name as it winds through rushes, though like most river names it has changed radically from its Celtic origins, possibly parallel to the Welsh Gwendraeth 'white strand'. Seen from the meadow Asthall can readily be appreciated as a topographical name, for the church and manor clearly shelter on the east side of a wooded bank.

Seek a stile to the left of some bushes among old gravel pit hollows, maintain course across the ensuing meadow to join a hedge-line to two stiles enclosing a stone slab. Proceed past a cottage on the left, reaching the road at a stile adjacent to the Swan Inn. Go right carefully round the sharp corner, passing a superb Cotswold barn, and keep left at the junction. Notice the delightful cottage garden walls and the curious witch weathervane.

Ascend the steps left into Swinbrook churchyard. Take the time to admire the table tombs and the clear glass east window pouring light upon the Tudor and Stuart Fettiplace monuments within the church. The Fettiplace mansion is lost along with the notable family line, but, leaving the churchyard by a narrow walled footpath on course for St Oswald's, the old terraced gardens and fishpond at the foot of the hill readily reveal its location. *Cross the stile in its midst and advance to a waymark post; ahead, beyond the cattle grid, is Widford Church.* It is seemingly remote from all habitation

but tell-tale hummocks in the adjacent pasture confirm the medieval 'lost' village. Within the church, box pews fill the nave, while the chancel harbours fragments of floor mosaic, indicating that this was the site of a Roman villa.

Returning to the waymark post ascend Dean Bottom via two new stiles onto a minor road. Go right to the brow of the hill branching left down a leafy lane. From the bridgegate veer right down the valley, but keep to the left of the rushes to avoid the springs on the right. Pass between a thorn bush and a fence, and slant right at a drystone wall. Cross over a little stream by a telegraph pole and continue straight to a gate onto the valley road. The road accompanies the clear stream passing attractive 17th- and 18th-century cottages into Swinbrook. The name 'swine brook' suggests the valley was once a ruder place in stark contrast with the pretty order of today. At this point you may retrace your steps to the car park through Swinbrook and Asthall or make a detour onto higher ground for a more scenic view of the Windrush valley.

Cross the stream beside the ford and go left up the hill, continuing out of the village onto Chalk Hill, then turn right and descend to Asthall Bridge. Take the opportunity of inspecting Asthall more closely, especially the church and Manor House, where Nancy Mitford and her sisters spent their childhood. The Redesdale family later moved to Swinbrook House at South Lawn. *Leaving the village via the beech avenue, retrace your steps up the road to Asthall Barrow car park.* The actual barrow, adorned with Scots pine is a prominent landmark and was raised as an early Saxon burial mound.

WALK 13
The
Barringtons

Allow 2¼ hours

This not too strenuous walk encompasses a trio of charming villages, a great mansion and the finest Cotswold freestone extracted from local 'quars' and used in London churches and Oxford colleges.

Park adjacent to the Windrush Eater (GR189125). Go right almost immediately and descend the unsignposted minor road off the A40, passing Glebe Farm, to the tiny tree-shaded green in front of Windrush Church. Take the time to look at the parish church, which encapsulates the essence of local style and form: Baroque table tombs, Perpendicular 'wool' tower and an early Norman south doorway carved with two complete rows of beakheads. The cottages to the north and east of the church make a delightful composition; notice particularly the pointed arch doorway, a 14th-century survival. (A further example is seen at Lower Cottages in Little Barrington.)

Go right where the road bends through a kissing gate, opening up a view of Barrington Park with the prominent Pigeon House. Cross the pasture to a gate followed by a fenced passage for cows, and continue onward via stone and wooden stiles into the lane next to Green Drive Farm house. Follow the lane around to the left, passing the post office. You can pay a visit to Little Barrington church by following the Upton (Middle) Road, but for many the visual charm of the upper terrace of cottages, each subtly different from its neighbour yet harmonious as a group, will be the real pleasure to savour. *Cross the foot of the sloping green and then the road to follow the byway onto a confined footpath. Go left across the River Windrush to reach Barrington Mill via the stile and lane.* The scene has been little trammelled by the march of time, indeed the image of a horse and wagon, trundling up loaded with sisal sacks of grist, is not hard to visualise.

Pass in front of the mill building and ascend the mill lane to Great Barrington. On meeting the road, turn right, passing the sadly neglected old school and village hall. Both are superb buildings crying out for use; neither at present having a role to play in a village bereft of youthful enterprise and vitality. From here there are lovely views of the Windrush valley. *Go left along the short path onto the main street.* Facing you, a completely restored cottage makes a striking contrast with the drab exteriors of most other houses. Architecturally, Great Barrington is assuredly homogenous, an estate village with little desire to forsake its agricultural roots, which gave it its identity, but in recent decades, with the swing away from a labour intensive industry, the village has lost its purpose though not its vernacular beauty. *Go left along the main street and then left again at the monument.* Take the opportunity of visiting St Mary's, a large Norman church with Bray and Talbot monuments. The great mansion adjoining it was built for Earl Talbot in 1736–8 by William Kent.

Descend beneath the high garden wall to cross the mill stream onto Strong's Causeway. This was named after Thomas Strong, master mason to Sir Christopher Wren, who left money in his will for the repair of this road for his funeral cortège in 1681. *The route passes the Fox Inn, the social centre of the neighbourhood. Go right along the road for Windrush. Look out for a stone stile on the right to take you on course for Windrush Mill, reached via three stiles. Go left up the mill lane, then left over a stone stile, with 'Windrush' marked on the step. Go straight across a paddock, over a stile and into a lane rising into Windrush village, going left on the road and returning up the narrow road right to the A40.*

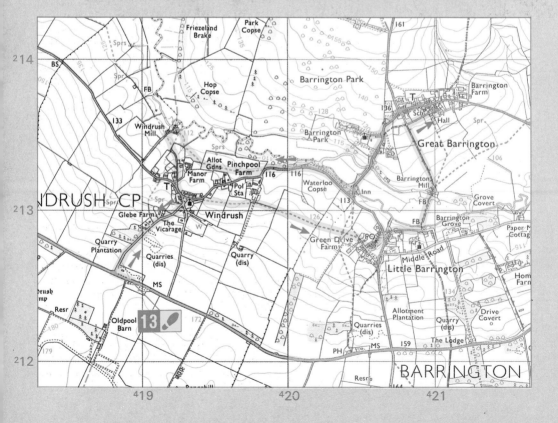

The Slaughters

Allow 2½ hours

A fairly leisurely walk, much of it on level ground, linking three of the most popular Cotswold villages.

Start from the large car park (GR171203) (small fee April to September) in Bourton-on-the-Water. Follow the path beside the river, cross the first bridge left and keep on the streamside path till the road bridge at the Motor Museum (former mill). Go right to the road junction and turn left. Turn right along the metalled path passing the parish church. In 1784 the Norman church, on Saxon foundations, was demolished, and a Georgian church was built onto the preserved chancel.

The tarmac footpath leads past Bourton Vale School left onto Station Road. Notice the canopied station building opposite. Turn right along the path beside the Foss Way (A429). Approaching the Coach and Horses cross the main road onto a tarmac footpath, which leads to Lower Slaughter across fields and enters the village along the east bank of Slaughter Brook. The 19th-century church now has its elegant spire capped with fibreglass and the 17th-century manor-house is now a hotel.

Keep with the stream and go towards the right past the Mill, Collett's Bakery and the post office, then turn left between the buildings. Go through two kissing gates, past the long millpond, then slant up over ridge-and-furrow pastureland via stiles and gates before descending to a short lane onto the road, right, at Upper Slaughter. Over the road bridge follow the road left, marked No Through Road, past some delightful cottages, then left over the footbridge by the ford and up the rise. Whilst paying a visit to the church notice the architectural touches of Edwin Lutyens evident in the nearby cottages, and the strangely sunken path. *From the triangular 'square' turn right to the road junction. The gate opposite leads onto a bridleway, which you ascend. At the top turn right through a gate and go diagonally across a field into a lane to the right of the farm. At the road junction turn left and follow Buckle Street past Brassey's Buildings.*

Continue along the road enjoying the fine view of Bourton Vale until a signposted bridleway lane forks right, descending via gates towards Aston Mill. At the foot of the lane, before entering Aston, go left to a gate, briefly following the old Banbury–Cheltenham railway, then over the Windrush meadows (passing through several gates). A stone plaque on Bourton Bridge commemorates the Roman Second Legion, who constructed this section of the Foss Way. *Follow Lansdown Road into Bourton-on-the-Water turning right at the footpath sign opposite Hill Cottage. Pass some delightful back gardens before going through kissing gates into the village street. Turn left past the Trendy Duke and retrace your steps down the main street to the car park.*

0	200	400	600	800	1		2		3	Kilometres

0	200	400	600	800	1000		1		2 Miles

SCALE 1:25000

WALK 15
Countryman Country

Allow 2½ hours

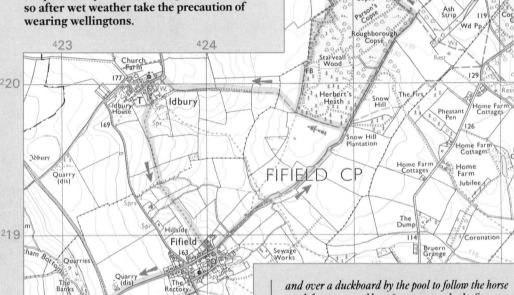

Three-horse ploughing team at work

A rural ramble over the oolitic limestone ridge via charming springline villages to explore pastures and woodland upon the lias clay. In the Nature Reserve some tracks are frequented by horses, making them muddy, so after wet weather take the precaution of wearing wellingtons.

Park at the layby (GR234182) on the A424 just south of the Merrymouth Inn. Go north towards the inn turning right through the gateway onto a bridleway track that leads over the skyline and down to the road to Fifield. Turn left, then first right past the parish church with its unusual 14th-century octagonal west tower. Swing left along the street, branching down right at the bridleway sign, and follow the lane to a gate proclaiming 'Fifield Parish Common'. Though the common land is no longer regularly grazed, it is invaluable as a wildlife habitat, notably for insects.

Approaching Herbert's Heath the lane narrows. After passing through a gate opt either to turn left along the south fringe of the woodland to a hunting gate and thence to Idbury, or continue along the path to explore Foxholes Nature Reserve. If you are daunted by the many paths in the wood, choose the shorter alternative route.

The open ride goes via Snow Hill and, after crossing a track, soon diminishes to a path that slips out of Roughborough Copse at a partially overgrown white gate. Now follow the edge of the woodland to a gate left, re-enter the wood continuing on the bridleway for 400 yards. Turn left at the path junction then fork right, shortly afterwards passing an old shepherd's hut. On reaching a path junction turn left to pass a hunting gate working round Wetpool Corner under the horse barrier

and over a duckboard by the pool to follow the horse track from a second hunting gate, or take the firmer path under the fence to a hardcore track, then turn right.

Whilst winding through Starveall Wood diverge from the track at a sharp left bend, to follow a confined path to the right, out of the wood. The path follows the wood south. Upon reaching the hunting gate (mentioned prior to entering Herbert's Heath) turn right, skirt round the headland to a gateway then cross the unploughed strip onto a track. On first glimpsing Idbury church, turn right at the gate, walk up the pasture to a double gate, then onto the road by the Old School House. An Iron Age hill-fort above the village is considered to be the origin of the placename 'Ida's Burg'. Idbury House, an imposing three-storeyed Tudor manor-house, was once the home of J W Robertson Scott, the original editor of *The Countryman* magazine. St Nicholas' is an appealing little church. Look for the blocked Norman north doorway and in the churchyard nearby a grandiose memorial to Sir Benjamin Baker, architect of the Forth Bridge.

Take the lane left from a post box, on reaching the wall stile go right, cross the tiny stream then slant diagonally across the ridge-and-furrow pasture to a gate. Continue via another gate before descending first to a concealed footbridge, located where the ridge and furrow alters orientation. Rise with the faint bank, pass through the old rank hedge and drop down to cross the next dingle via two hunting gates. Continue across the long pasture to reach a metal kissing gate, and proceed along the confined path to another kissing gate leading into Fifield. Turn right, passing the village post office/shop, continue straight on at the village crossroads until reaching the junction by the Merrymouth Inn, cross over the road, then turn left to reach your car.

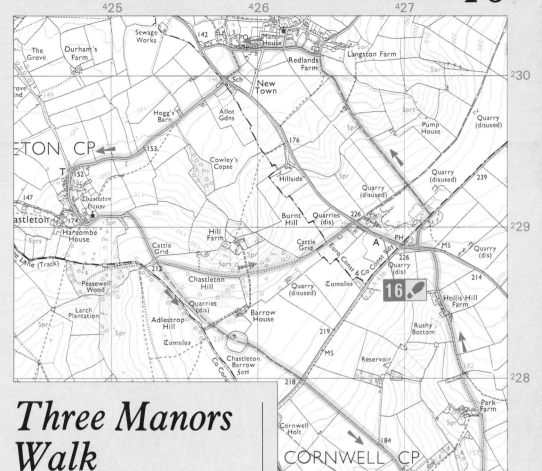

Three Manors Walk

Allow 2¾ hours

A walk blessed with fine views and three striking manor-houses.

Park at the layby (GR269289) west of the Cross Hands Inn, walk back past the inn taking the minor road left, signposted Rollrights. From Neolithic times it would appear that the continuous spine of hill country constituting the Cotswolds offered a dry ridgeway route for travel and trade; the road you are now following is part of this route. *Two hundred and fifty yards on the left a hunting gate (bridleway sign) gives access to a track leading north-west past Newman's Quarry.* Ahead is a superb view revealing Ilmington Downs, Dover's Hill, Batsford Hill and Bourton Downs with the Vale of the Stour leading north towards Stratford-upon-Avon.

The bridleway descends for ¾ mile; on entering Little Compton through a gate, turn left along the minor road. Do take the trouble of inspecting the parish church of St Denys (second turning right) adjacent to the very fine manor-house.

Return to the street going right, until you reach the wicket gate left, close to the telephone box. A tarmac path leads to a kissing gate, the route crosses the A44 at the primary school with its distinctive monkey puzzle tree. Proceed along the quiet road to Chastleton, turning left at the junction. Chastleton has several attractive thatched cottages and farmhouses, but Chastleton House transcends all in its magnificence. Built soon after 1602 by the wool merchant Walter Jones, this Jacobean masterpiece, still privately owned, has frequently been used for period film locations, but is not open to the public.

Continue up the road to a sharp corner junction, cross the cattle grid left then the stile immediately right. Alternatively at this point the walk can be shortened by simply following the unenclosed road directly to the Cross Hands Inn. Ascend the pasture, admiring the view north featuring Brailes Hill with the spinney on top. Advancing parallel with the county boundary road, go through the gate onto the Barrow House drive, turning left then first right over a gate, following the fence to a metal gate into Chastleton Barrow. It is thought that this Iron Age hill-fort was the origin of the parish name.

Pass diagonally through the circular tree-fringed earthwork, the perfect cricketing arena, to a further metal gate. The bridleway follows the hedge down to the A436 (Jurassic Way). Go down the single track road to Cornwell with views east to Chipping Norton and south to Churchill. Where the road bends, after the sawmill, follow the track left, branching right diagonally across the apple orchard, shielded by a tall hedge, to a kissing gate. Turn sharp right down the field to join the fenced path to the church where the metal fencing begins. In 1936 Clough Williams-Ellis was given liberty to re-model the estate village, together with much of the manor-house, bringing elaborate formal gardens and vistas to beautify a fine setting.

Descend the parkland pasture to a passage between gates over a bridge, rising to a further kissing gate into a lane. Go left to conclude the walk via Hollis Hill.

Index

Page numbers in bold type indicate main entries.

Acknowledgements

The publishers would like to thank the many individuals who helped in the preparation of this book. Special thanks are due to the Cotswold Voluntary Warden Service and the Nature Conservancy Council.

The lines from 'Crickley Hill' by Ivor Gurney on page 10 are taken from the *Collected Poems of Ivor Gurney* edited by PJ Kavanagh 1984 and reproduced by permission of Oxford University Press.

The extract from the hymn tune 'Down Ampney' by Ralph Vaughan Williams (1872–1958) is taken from the *English Hymnal* and reproduced by permission of Oxford University Press.

The Automobile Association wishes to thank the following photographers, organisations and libraries for their assistance in the compilation of this book. Many of the photographs reproduced are the copyright of the AA Picture Library.

Cider Mill Gallery 71 Horse-drawn mill; *Corinium Museum* 22/3 Pavement; *Cotswold Countryside Collection* 62 Roof Tiles, 116 Plough Horses; *Cotswold Farm Park* 52; *Cotswold Water Park* 64; *PW Dixon* 10 Long Barrow, 11 Crickley Hill, 24 Stoke Orchard, 24/5 Little Rissington, 35 Gt Coxwell; *SJ Dorey* Cover Upper Slaughter, 18/19 Nr Bibury, 43 Butter Market, 75 Saintbury; *Gloucester City Museum* 12 Birdlip; *Gloucester, Shire Hall* 9 Bisley, Cooper's Hill, 10 Hetty Pegler's Tump, 17 Farmland, 19 Ceramics, 20 Foss Way, 26 Cottages, 28 Cotswold Way, 30/1 Cam Long Down, 31 North Nibley, 32 Stanton, 39 Tree Planting, 47 Cooper's Hill, 63 Snowshill, 64 Cokes Pit Anglers, 69 Winchcombe, 70 Donnington, 72/3 Cranham Feast, 73 Horse Fair; *Heart of England Tourist Board* 8 Owlpen, 32 Church, 35 Little Barrington, 36 Berkeley, 101 Eastleach; *A Lawson* 51 Docks, 64 Stanton, 65 Stanway; *June Lewis* 43 Chipping Campden; *Susan Lund* 27 Morris Men; *Mary Evans Picture Library* 44 Pavement, 48 Vaughan Williams, 105 Lych Gate, 106 Farmyard, 108 Painswick, 109 Stile, 110 Kissing Gate; *S & O Matthews* 3 Gloucester, 23 Coin, 27 Broadway, 33 Tewkesbury, 34 Ampney St Mary, 36 Bath, 37 Blockley, 38 Bourton-on-the-Water, Bourton-on-the-Hill, 39 Bredon Hill, 40 Broadway CP, 41 Burford, Castle Combe, 44 Cirencester, 45 Cleeve Hill, 46 Cold Aston, Coaley Peak, 47 Coln St Dennis, 48 Crickley Hill, 49 Down Ampney, Dursley, 50 Dyrham Park, Filkins, 51 Gloucester, 53 Sign, House, 55 Lechlade, 56 Minchinhampton, Minster Lovell, 57 Leckhampton, Moreton-in-Marsh, 58 Nailsworth, Vet's Box, 59 Painswick, Prestbury, 60/1 Rollrights, 63 Lower Slaughter, 65 Stow-on-the-Wold, 66 Stroud, Sudeley, 67 Kiftsgate, 68 Westonbirt, 69 Witney, 70 Wotton-under-Edge, 96 Fruit and Vegetable Stall, 100 Cirencester Buscot Park, 101 Fairford; *Museum of English Rural Life* Back cover Farm Wagon, 45 Ewe; *Nature Photographers* 13 Stonechat (T Andrewartha), Yellow Hammer (C Carver), 14 Tawny Owl (H Clark), Early Purple Orchid (D Bonsall), 15 Bird's-Foot-Trefoil, Peacock Butterfly (P Sterry), 16 Kingfisher (P Sterry); *Sporting Pictures* 72/3 Steeplechasers; *R Surman* 21 Chedworth, 42 Roman Mosaic, 54 Hidcote Manor, Pool Garden, 67 Tetbury, Snowshill; *H Williams* 37 Arlington Row, 52 & 53 Hailes Abbey Museum, 99 Hailes Abbey; *T Wood* 5 Chipping Campden, 40 View from Tower, 97 Hidcote, 99 Lower Slaughter, *John Wyand* 6/7 Crickley Hill, 42 Cheltenham.

Other Ordnance Survey Maps of the Cotswolds

How to get there with Routemaster and Routeplanner Maps

Reach the Cotswolds from Birmingham, London, Cardiff and Southampton using Ordnance Survey Routemaster Map Sheets 7, 8, and 9. Alternatively use the Ordnance Survey Routeplanner Map which covers the whole country and is updated annually.

Exploring with the Landranger and Tourist Maps

Landranger Series	Tourist Map Series
1¼ inches to one mile or 1:50 000 scale	1 inch to one mile or 1:63 360 scale

These maps cover the whole of Britain and are good for local motoring and walking. Each contains tourist information such as parking, picnic places, viewpoints and rights of way. Sheets covering the Cotswolds are:	These maps cover popular holiday areas and are ideal for discovering the countryside. In addition to normal map detail ancient monuments, camping and caravan sites, parking facilities and viewpoints are marked. Lists of selected places of interest are included on some sheets and others include useful guides to the area.

150 Worcester & the Malverns
151 Stratford-upon-Avon
163 Cheltenham & Cirencester
164 Oxford
172 Bristol & Bath
173 Swindon & Devizes

Tourist Map Sheet 8 covers the Cotswolds.